Exploring the Greek Mosaic

A Guide to Intercultural Communication in Greece

Benjamin J. Broome

Exploring the Greek Mosaic

A GUIDE TO INTERCULTURAL COMMUNICATION IN GREECE

Benjamin J. Broome

INTERCULTURAL PRESS, INC.

First published by Intercultural Press. For information, contact:

Intercultural Press, Inc.	Nicholas Brealey Publishing
PO Box 700	36 John Street
Yarmouth, Maine 04096, USA	London, WC1N 2AT, UK
207-846-5168	44-207-430-0224
Fax: 207-846-5181	Fax: 44-207-404-8311
www.interculturalpress.com	www.nbrealey-books.com

© 1996 by Benjamin J. Broome

Book design and production by Patty J. Topel
Cover illustration and design by Patty J. Topel
Mosaic pattern taken from the House of Dionysos, a late second-/ early third-century Greco-Roman house excavated in Nea Paphos in Cyprus.

Printed in the United States of America

04   03   02   01   00   2   3   4   5   6

Library of Congress Cataloging-in-Publication Data

Broome, Benjamin J.
    Exploring the Greek mosaic : a guide to intercultural communication in Greece / Benjamin J. Broome.
       p. cm.
    Includes bibliographical references and index.
    ISBN 1-877864-39-0
    1. Intercultural communication—Greece.   2. Greece— Civilization.   3. United States—Relations—Greece. 4. Greece—Relations—United States.   I. Title.
P94.65.G8B76   1996
949.5—dc
                                    95-52223
                                      CIP

Acknowledgments

I am grateful to all those who contributed their thoughts and support to this book, including the following people:

Aliki Bafilia, Yiorgos Bafilias, John Bailey, Gordon Ball, George Besi, John Bilimatsis, Diana Chigas, Aleco Christakis, James Clambaneva, Wess and Marylin DuBrisk, Argyro Efthimiou, Sloane Elliot, Susanne Gosselin, Mike Hemovich, Petter Hennum, Herakles Ipiotis, Zoe Karantzalis, Stathis Kormentzas, Dimitrios Koutsodimitropoulos, Ioulietta Laouri-Kalli, Vasili Liarakos, Michael Lowy, Theodore Lyras, Nikolas Manticas, Anastasios Marcos, Demetria Moran, Don Munn, David Neighbor, Vassiliki (Kiki) Nikiforidou, Rena and Madeleine Pappas, Nikos Pirounakis, Andreas Poulakis, John Priamou, George Salimbene, Tom Scotes, Phillip Sell, Costas Sophoulis, Lykis Spartiotis, Nicos Tatsis, Symeon Tsomokos, Paris Tsoukalas, Viola Tzortziopoulou, Eleni Varika, George

Vayatis, James Williams, Lillian Yamasaki, Christos Zeris, and others who did not wish to have their names included.

Special thanks go to my families in Greece—Velissarios, Ditsa, and Myrka Anthes; and Ioannes, Katerina, and Iris Kapelouzos—who have offered me their homes for extended periods of time while in Athens. I especially appreciate the generous offer of Ioanna Varika, who allowed me to use her son's garden apartment in Athens to finish my writing during the summer of 1994. Its expansive view of the Saronic Gulf, Mt. Imitos, and the Acropolis, along with the wonderful light that flooded its interior throughout the day, provided me much inspiration and energy at a critical point in my writing. Patrick Leigh Fermor read an early draft of the manuscript and gave me encouragement to continue. I thankfully acknowledge George Mason University for granting me a semester study leave to complete the manuscript, and I especially appreciate the support and encouragement of Don Boileau, my department chair.

I thoroughly enjoyed working with the staff of Intercultural Press, particularly David Hoopes, whose detailed editing and insightful comments gave clarity and coherence to the manuscript and simultaneously taught me much about good writing style.

Finally, I wish to express my deep gratitude to my lifelong companion, Bliss Little, my partner and colleague during my experiences in *Ellada* (Greece), whose presence and inspiration provided strength for staying the course during an uncertain journey through an unpredictable landscape.

Table of Contents

Preface

Making generalizations about Greeks is not an easy task. I am sure that many Greek readers will disagree with some of the statements I have made about their culture. The difficulty of describing cultural patterns in a manner that does not distort reality is one that challenges any writer who dares to enter a world that is not his or her own. Generalizations are inherently misleading, yet without them the human mind cannot survive the onslaught of incoming stimuli that results from new experiences. This creates a dilemma about how best to present observations and hypotheses about other cultures.

My own response to this issue is not a simple one, but it allows me to seek general cultural patterns while avoiding putting individuals into preconceived molds or stereotypes. The key lies in learning what it is that people in the society consider *appropriate* and *acceptable*. In those cases when I am talking with someone who does not exhibit a particular cultural attitude or behavior, he or she may nevertheless consider it appropriate and acceptable for others to do so. If several people are surprised by a conclusion that I have formed about the culture, then it is likely that I am mistaken. If there is general consensus, however, that such an attitude or behavior is appropriate and acceptable within the society, then

I can be more confident in making a statement about cultural characteristics.

I believe it is best to view culture as a vast reservoir of values, attitudes, and communication patterns that exist within a society, and from which its people obtain the nourishment that shapes their own worldview and their understanding of what is appropriate behavior. As individuals grow up in a society, they draw from this reservoir to form their own character and personality. However, the reservoir is much too large for any one person to partake of its full range of content, and people are selectively exposed to only certain parts of the whole; even when exposed to the same content, people usually respond in different ways. Although there is a certain consistency and congruence among the various elements making up the reservoir, there are competing elements, sometimes resulting in contradictions and paradoxes. In addition, some people have access to other reservoirs from other societies. Finally, the reservoir itself is constantly being replenished with fresh waters from the various streams that feed into the main body of values, attitudes, and behavior patterns. In today's global society, these feeder streams are certainly not "pristine waters." Some of them are polluted, and some of them have been enriched with nutrients from afar.

In reading the pages of this book, it is best to view my descriptions of Greek culture as trail markers that provide direction rather than as the reality you will encounter. This guide can help you map your journey, and it can assist you in understanding the episodes along the way. It cannot guarantee success, but it can serve as a starting point for dialogue with the many people that I hope you will meet during your own exploration of the Greek mosaic.

1

Introduction: Images of Greece

When I ask friends or acquaintances to describe their images of contemporary *Ellada*, better known to English language speakers as the country of Greece,[1] their portrayals usually center on either Greek antiquity, island beaches, or a leaping Zorba. Most can readily point to contributions of fifth-century B.C. Greeks to the development of Western civilization: Athens is cited as the birthplace of Western democracy; Greeks are credited with the invention of Western logic, mathematics, and science; and Greek art and philosophy are referred to as the basis of Western civilization. Travelers from Europe, the United States, Canada, and Australia come by the hundreds of thousands each year to visit the Acropolis and its magnificent Parthenon, to see the Greek statues and vases on display in the museums, and to walk the streets of the *agora*[2] (marketplace), where Socrates, Plato, and Aristotle conversed with the people of ancient Athens.

Accompanying these historical images are mental pictures of the sun, sea, and villages of the Greek islands. Indeed, thousands crowd the beaches of the Greek shores each year, enjoying the brilliant sunlight, the tranquil waters, and the refreshing breezes of *kalokeri* (summer), under the limitless Greek sky that Patrick Leigh Fermor described as "higher and lighter and which surrounds one closer and stretches further

1

into space than anywhere else in the world."³ During the day, sun worshipers soak up the therapeutic rays of the Mediterranean sunshine, and at night tourists fill the *tavernas* (restaurants) lining the waterfronts of fishing villages. They leisurely pass the evening consuming simple but savory food cooked in olive oil and garlic, seasoned with herbs gathered from the mountains, and served with fresh seasonal fruits.

Complementing these visions of island paradise are stereotypes of the Greek character. While most of my friends have personally known few, if any, Greeks as individuals, almost all have seen the movie *Zorba the Greek*. They readily recall his zest for life in the face of adversity and his attempts to help his stiff English employer free himself from the chains of worry. We think immediately of the music, dance, and carefree attitude portrayed in this film, and we expect all Greeks to exhibit the character of Zorba.

In magazines, tourist brochures, postcards, movies, and textbooks these images of Greece are spread to Europe, North America, and elsewhere, inviting all to visit what the Greek National Tourist Organization calls the "Land Chosen by the Gods." In response, approximately six million tourists visit Greece each year, including nearly one-half million from the United States. Unfortunately, few people understand much about the people, culture, and traditions of contemporary Greece. Tourists are often surprised to find Athens a bustling, modern city, facing problems common to all urban areas: traffic jams, pollution, shortage of open space, and limited room to expand. The ancient statues and paintings of Hermes, Poseidon, Aphrodite, and Demeter provide tourists with few clues to understanding the people of modern Greece. New arrivals feel confused and caught up in chaos, suspecting that they have mistakenly arrived in Lebanon, Turkey, or a Middle Eastern country. At first glance, Greece seems far from the "birthplace of Western civilization."

The incomplete picture we hold of Greece is due in part to a lack of information and attention. While textbooks on philosophy, art, and science in the West generally present a great deal of information about the Greeks of antiquity, they rarely mention postclassical Greece. For example, we read in our history books that the early Christian church split into East and West in the fourth century, but we learn very little about the Eastern church after that time. Few realize the extent of its empire or the advances in intellectual thought that occurred in the East between the formal division of the Roman Empire in A.D. 395 and the fall of Constantinople in 1453. For over a thousand years, the Byzantine Empire flourished, while in the West the Dark Ages set in. Similarly, we learn about the war between Athens and Sparta in the fifth century B.C., but we are unaware of the Greek war for independence from the Ottomans[4] that started in 1821 and resulted in the birth of Greece as a nation. Most of us do not know that Greeks were under the rule of the Ottoman Empire for four hundred years and that they struggled during this time to maintain their language and customs. In like manner, we learn very little from our World War II history books about the brutal German occupation of Greece, and we are almost totally unaware of the divisive civil war that followed. Even today, our newspapers report practically nothing about events in Greece, unless hijackings or terrorist bombings occur. Thus, when we visit Greece, we find ourselves almost completely ignorant of the issues that fill the daily newspapers and conversations in the homes and *kafenia* (coffee shops).

Another basic factor that contributes to the lack of information about Greece in the United States is the relatively minor importance placed on its economic and military position in the spectrum of U.S. relations with the rest of the world. Prior to the Second World War, the United States and Greece had few political ties. In 1947 the Truman Doctrine opened a new era in U.S. relations with Greece. U.S. economic aid played a key role in Greece's recovery from the German occupation of World War II, while U.S. military aid provided the means for the Greek Nationalist forces to defeat the Communist army in its struggle for control of Greece. Yet as late as 1974 Greece was still not part of the European Bureau of the U.S. State Department. Instead, it was located in the Near East section, where Iranian, Arab, and Israeli relations dominated the attention of top officials. Only in a few instances, such as the assumption of power by the military junta in 1967 or the Turkish military intervention in Cyprus in 1974, has Greece received significant attention from the U.S. government.

Of course, it is unfair to imply that Greece holds no importance to the United States. It is well known that ideas of a republican democracy are based in part on the democratic practices of ancient Athens, but most people are not aware that Greek was a candidate in the early Congress as the official language of the United States. The new government, seeking to differentiate itself from England, is said to have defeated by a single vote a measure that would have resulted in the transaction of all government business in Greek.[5] Although it did not become the official language, Greek nevertheless permeates our everyday speech in ways of which we are not aware. Of the nearly 166,000 words in Webster's *International Dictionary of the English Language*, over 41,000, or 25 percent of the total, are of Greek origin. Of the approximately 40,000 words in our vernacular speech, over 5,000 are based on the Greek language. In specialized scientific fields, particularly medicine, nearly 50 percent of the terminology is Greek.[6]

Greece borders on Albania, Bulgaria, and the former Yugoslavian state of Macedonia and, along with its neighbor Turkey, forms the southeastern flank of NATO. During times when Soviet aggression was perceived as a threat, Greece held a great deal of strategic importance. The United States has maintained military bases in Greece over the years, although most of these were closed in 1990 and 1991. The U.S. State Department estimates that there are over three million persons of Greek descent living in the United States,[7] and a strong Greek lobby has continuously made sure that Greece is not forgotten in matters of military aid.

Greece draws people from the United States for many different reasons. Students of history, archeology, and art come to Greece to visit and study at libraries, excavations, and museums. Honeymooners and retired couples book cruises in the Aegean. Sun worshipers rent rooms and villas near the beach on islands such as Rhodes, Crete, Santorini, Samos, and Corfu. Mythology buffs roam the countryside, looking for the valley of the Muses, the entrance to Hades, and the Eleusinian mysteries. Educational exchange programs bring students for a year abroad. Government and military officials call upon their Greek counterparts. Representatives of business interests are assigned to Greece to manage employees. Thousands of second- and third-generation Greeks make the pilgrimage to a homeland which they know about only from grandparents' stories. Finally, approximately 60,000 U.S. citizens call Greece home, living and working in the country for periods ranging from one year to a lifetime.

While there are numerous incentives for visiting or living in Greece, it is a common experience that the Westerner finds the country and its people confusing and perplexing. People describe Greece as a tangled web in which it is easy to become snarled, or a complicated puzzle that is impossible to decipher. Why, people ask, should the birthplace of Western civilization be so difficult for the Westerner to comprehend? Do the Greeks of today bear any resemblance to what we know of Socrates, Plato, Aristotle, and other citizens of ancient Athens? On several occasions when I have described the traffic, the bureaucracy, the pollution, the political disarray, and the sprawling concrete jungle that make up today's Athens, people beg me to stop destroying their image of Athens as a quiet Mediterranean city of coffee shops with calm, easygoing citizens preoccupied with art, philosophy, and music. Indeed, my own initial experiences in Greece were both confusing and disconfirming of the stereotypes that I held.

When I first lived in Greece (in 1980), I decided to attend a performance in the Herod Atticus Theater that lies at the base of the Acropolis. The bus route from my apartment in the northern suburb of Aghia Paraskevi ended in the center of Athens, from where I intended to walk a short distance through the old Plaka area of Athens to reach the Acropolis. Using a map of the city center as my guide, I set out through the old section of the city. While the map displayed a complex array of small streets, I was confident that I would find my way easily, since I simply had to keep heading in a southeasterly direction to reach my destination. I expected the height of the Acropolis would be constantly visible to help me keep my orientation. Much to my dismay, I immediately became lost. The streets twisted and turned, sometimes ending altogether, and none of them followed a straight line. Street names, where they happened to be posted, were usually written in the Greek script, and my knowledge of the language was only in the beginning stages. My attempts to ask directions were fruitless, in part because I had difficulty understanding the replies, but also because the directions themselves involved too many spins and pivots. Occasionally I caught sight of the Acropolis sitting high above the maze in which I was trapped, but it seemed that I was getting no closer. Finally, I arrived at the base of the hill on which the ancient monument stood, only to find that I couldn't reach the other side, where the theater was located, since the gate that allowed me direct access was locked. When I finally arrived at the theater, the performance was half over, and my self-confidence was destroyed. I had entered an unknown world, and now I understood why Theseus needed Ariadne's help in finding his way out of the Minoan labyrinth so long ago. Fortunately, there had been no minotaurs to slay along the way!

To the North American and European visitor, Greece is baffling, indecipherable to one looking for a strictly Western sense of order. In his insightful book *Greece without Columns*, David Holden described the country as a "maddening mobile, elusive, paradoxical world, where there seems nothing solid enough to grasp save splinters, yet where no part is less than the mystical whole and where past and present, body and soul, ideal and reality blend and struggle and blend again with each other so that the most delicate scalpel can scarcely dissect them."[8] Contrary to initial impressions, however, the Greek world is not a labyrinth but rather a *mosaic*. The combination of diverse elements that make up Greek society form a pattern that may be difficult to decipher but that is integrated into a meaningful paradigm. However, in order for the mosaic to reveal itself, the traveler must be willing to climb the winding, twisting, meandering, and often tortuous paths that lead through the Greek landscape. One must understand that this pattern did not arise from a neatly drawn design, but like the streets of the Plaka, it developed over a long period of time through demanding circumstances.

Thus, the paths of the Greek social landscape are short and narrow, with numerous twists and turns. The newcomer is easily lost, but with sufficient time and effort one is able to establish a sense of direction that keeps one from losing the way. However, it is important to heed the words of the famous Greek poet Constantinos Cavafy, who says:

As you set out on your journey to Ithaki,
wish the way to be long,
full of adventures, full of discovery.[9]

It is from these experiences, he believes, that riches are gained, not from what awaits at the journey's end. In a similar manner, the most important part of one's sojourn in Greece is the interpersonal encounters that occur while navigating the relational domain. While many difficulties and frustra-

tions will be confronted, exciting adventures await the traveler who adopts a posture of openness and a learning attitude
toward those one meets on the way.

The chapters that follow are intended to help the reader
develop increased sensitivity to the Greek way of life and a
solid basis for cultivating meaningful relationships with Greek
neighbors, acquaintances, and colleagues. In this guide are
many generalizations about different aspects of Greek society
and the characteristics of its people. As is the case in any
culture, no single individual in Greece will fit the mold of
these descriptions. We have all been influenced in different
ways by our cultures. Just as importantly, there are numerous
exceptions to the general cultural patterns presented in this
book. I know many people who exhibit exactly the opposite
characteristics from those described here.[10] In Greece, perhaps more than in most places in the world, there are sharply
contrasting patterns of behavior within the society and often
even within the same individual. Finally, it is impossible to
predict the effect of the rapid changes occurring in Greece at
this moment, particularly those that result from increased
Western influence. While it is possible that only the outward
appearance of the culture will change, it is also possible that
the underlying value structure may be forever altered.

In this book I have based my observations about Greek
culture on a combination of field notes, interviews, and the
writings of anthropologists, sociologists, and travelers. In
addition, I have passed countless evenings in tavernas and in
the homes of friends and acquaintances, discussing my observations with Greek academics, educators, and other friends.
However, the material presented in this guide must be seen as
a reflection of the author's experiences and perceptions, not
as a description of Greek reality. Such a description would be
impossible to capture on paper, since reality must be experienced in the context of everyday life.

In many ways what is described here is a personal journey
through the Greek landscape, undertaken by one who has

participated as fully as possible in Greek life, yet who stands outside looking at the larger picture from a distance. As participant I experience the Greek way of life, and as observer I reflect on what I have seen and felt. I find that I must move in and out constantly between these positions, unable as either participant or observer to adequately comprehend the whole. In this small book I have sought to capture the essence of my experience and my reflection in the anticipation that others may benefit from my journey. I hope the information and impressions I share with you in the following pages may serve to increase the richness of your own experiences and help you decipher some of the complexities that you encounter in your own exploration of the Greek mosaic.

---

[1] The name *Greece* comes from the Latin term given by the Romans during their occupation of Greece. Greeks refer to their country as *Ellada*. The official name for the country is the Hellenic Republic. Because of its widespread usage, the term *Greece* will be used in this book.

[2] Greek terms used in the text are listed in the Glossary, with the appropriate Greek spelling. There exist several conventions for transliterating Greek words into the Latin script, and all of them are less than satisfactory for ease in understanding by the general public. Please note that when written in Greek, words always include (in lowercase only) a tone mark over the accented syllable. Rather than providing this tone mark for the Latin equivalents used in the text, I have included the Greek spellings in the Glossary.

[3] Patrick Leigh Fermor, *Mani: Travels in the Southern Peloponnese* (London: Penguin Books, 1958), 129.

[4] The Ottoman Empire began in A.D. 1300. The Ottomans are most often identified with Turkish-speaking people, although the empire included many lands.

[5] This event has been related to me by several Greek academics, although I have not been able to locate a written source to verify it. What is known is that the early Congress considered adopting a language other than English, and since Thomas Jefferson (and others) were versed in ancient Greek, this language was a candidate.

[6] Aristides E. Constantinides, in his book *Οι Ελληνικές Λέξεις στην Αγγλική Γλώσσα* (Thessaloniki: Aristides Constantinides, Karaiskaki 27, Thessaloniki 56626, 1993), has compiled a dictionary of all Greek words in the English language.

[7] *Background Notes: Greece* (U. S. Department of State, Bureau of Public Affairs, April 1985).

[8] David Holden, *Greece without Columns: The Making of the Modern Greeks* (Philadelphia: J. B. Lippincott, 1972), 34.

[9] See the full translation of *Ithaki* in the Postscript.

[10] See the author's note on methodology in the Preface.

2

Looking Forward to the Past

One evening I was sitting with a friend on his balcony in the
late afternoon, enjoying the sunset with a glass of *ouzo* (aperitif) and the accompanying *mezedes* (snacks). Our discussion
centered on the future of Greece and the importance of its
long history in shaping what will come. My friend is a highly
educated person, serving as a judge in the civil court system
and thus steeped in the history of Greece. He comes from a
traditional town in the central part of the country. As we
talked, I noticed that he usually pointed forward with his
hands when he wanted to indicate the past and gestured
behind when he referred to the future. I took the three glasses
of ouzo that we had on our table and arranged them in a line
stretching away from him, asking him to indicate which of
these glasses he considered to be the present, past, and future.
As I would have done, he pointed to the middle glass and
labeled it the present. However, the glass that was placed to
the front he designated as the past, and the one bringing up
the rear he declared the future. When I asked him to explain
this arrangement, he replied that the past is in front of us
because we can see it clearly, while the future is unknown
and lies behind our line of vision. As we move through time,
the future becomes the present and eventually part of the
past that can be viewed with understanding.

While few Greeks will arrange glasses of ouzo as my friend did that afternoon, almost everyone in Greece places a great deal of importance on the long and multilayered history of the country. As the gifted writer Nikos Kazantzakis wrote, "Pause on a patch of Greek earth and anguish overcomes you. It is a deep, twelve-level tomb, from which voices rise up calling to you."[1] This past is both a burden and a resource, weighing particularly heavy on relations between Greece and her Balkan and Turkish neighbors while simultaneously offering every Greek a sense of pride and strength. The interaction of past and present conditions the Greek mind and shapes the social behavior of Greek people. Unfortunately, outside of the country there is little awareness of the important issues that Greeks face or events that have shaped the country's present. Before one can understand Greek social relations or communication patterns, it is important to learn something about the country and the major issues that confront individuals on a daily basis.

The Setting

Geographically situated between Western Europe and Asia Minor, Greece occupies the southern tip of the Balkan Peninsula, jutting into the Mediterranean. The landmass consists of approximately 50,000 square miles and includes more than 1,600 islands, the majority of them located in the Aegean Sea between the Greek mainland and Turkey. Although tourist posters always depict a warm Mediterranean climate, there are four clearly distinguishable seasons throughout Greece, with winter bringing heavy snowfall in the higher elevations and hard, driving rain and rough seas in the coastal areas. Anyone who has formed an image of Greece based on the enticing posters put out by the Greek National Tourist Organization will be confronted with a rude awakening upon arrival in Greece during the late fall, winter, or early spring months.

The climate and environment are very important factors in shaping the character of Greeks. Several versions exist of a creation story that goes something like the following: When God had finished with his arrangement of all the places around the world, he had a large pile of unused rocks remaining. He wasn't sure what to do with them, so he just let them go from his hand and they fell into the sea. The place where they fell became the Greek peninsula. Indeed, it is not hard to see why Greece is often described as a rocky finger of the Balkans that extends boldly into the Mediterranean Sea. Even though there are dense forests, lush valleys, and beautiful lakes in Greece, the two primary characteristics of the landscape are rocky mountains and sea.[2] With its multitude of gulfs and numerous islands, the coastline is nearly as long as that of the United States, despite a land area no bigger than states such as Ohio or Alabama.

The population of Greece is approximately ten million people. There is not a great deal of ethnic diversity, with 97 percent of the population identifying themselves as Greek Orthodox. A small Muslim minority lives in the northeast province of Thrace, and recently there has been an influx of refugees from Albania to the northwest. Although there is currently an attempt to settle them into permanent villages, there are a substantial number of Gypsy bands roaming the Greek countryside.

Greece is linguistically homogeneous, even though throughout the nineteenth and twentieth centuries there have been significant disputes over the proper form of the language for use in schools, churches, literature, and for official documents. At one point students in school had to learn one form of the Greek language for everyday communication, another for reading newspapers, another for reading ancient literature, and still another for understanding the church service. Today, a single form of both spoken and written Greek is used, called *dimotiki*, although church liturgy still uses *koine*, the New Testament Greek of 2,000 years ago.

The Greeks are among the few people in the world, including the Israelis and Chinese, who can visit archeological sites that are nearly 3,000 years old and find their language used in the inscriptions. Of course, many changes have taken place in the language since ancient times, and it is only those who have studied the ancient tongue who can fully understand the meaning of these engraved words. However, the connection between modern Greek and the language of Homer in 1000 B.C. is still much stronger than is today's English with its much younger Old English roots.

The modern country of Greece is relatively young, having become a nation-state in 1831, following its struggle for independence from the Ottoman Empire. For most of its short history as a state, Greece was a constitutional monarchy known as the "Kingdom of Greece," with a king who came from Europe. Although the king had been deposed several times previously, it was only in 1974 that the people of Greece voted to permanently end the monarchy and become the Hellenic Republic. Politically, Greece is organized as a parliamentary republic under a president as the titular head of state and a prime minister as head of government. Justice is administered by an independent judiciary, which is divided into civil, criminal, and administrative courts.

Greece signed a membership agreement with the European Economic Community (which later became the European Union) in 1961 and was admitted as its tenth member in 1981. It has been the beneficiary of large sums invested by the Community, resulting in significant improvements in rural areas. Economically, Greece is far better off than its Balkan neighbors, but it lags far behind the other members of the European Union. It is at the bottom in per capita income, lowest in productivity, highest in inflation rate, and has the largest external debt, despite the fact that it receives over four billion dollars from the European Union each year for various projects. In spite of its poor economy, there is little poverty in Greece, and the educational level is high. Tourism

and shipping, as well as remittances from emigrés, bring in
the most money to the Greek economy.[3]

The Greek Approach to History

Greeks are often surprised by foreigners' lack of awareness of
crucial events in their own history. Particularly in the United
States, there is very little concern with the past. Despite the
fact that their nation's history goes back only three to four
hundred years, most U.S. citizens cannot discuss their
country's historical events in any detail. Additionally, almost
no one knows anything about the rich history of the native
tribes that preceded the formation of the nation-state in the
eighteenth century. Few people believe the past is important
enough to warrant much of their attention.

In contrast, most foreigners are impressed by the high
degree of awareness that most Greeks have of their own
history and by how often reference is made to these events in
conversation. However, the Greek view of the past is unlike
that normally held in the Western world. If asked to give an
account of past events, most Westerners will recite a linear
sequence of events that starts at a point in some distant past
and progresses through a series of events to the present time.
History thus becomes a row of milestones that shows progress
and advancement, with an occasional decline where there is
a dip in the road. The assumption is that things will continue
to get better as we travel along this straight road into the
future. There is great belief in the legitimacy of the written
record, such that once events are captured on the pages of
history texts, they are viewed as relatively indisputable facts.
In contrast, the listener will rarely hear Greeks describe an
orderly sequence of events, particularly in casual conversation. Instead, the speaker may discuss several events simultaneously, with "facts" and ideas constantly changing shape. As
Holden says, Greek discussion of history is "all jumbled up
together instead, like certain modern paintings and most

Byzantine icons. Everything remains in the foreground, as it were; everything is potentially of equal importance and everything is always relevant..., a cross between a kaleidoscope and a seamless web."[4]

Defining Moments in Recent Greek History

The written history of Greece dates from the time of Herodotos in the sixth century B.C., and archeological records show an unbroken record that goes back to at least the second millennium B.C., a spread of nearly 5,000 years involving a very complicated set of events. Throughout their long past, Greeks have been in constant conflict with one another. Just as the land is more divided than united, so too have the people more often found themselves in conflict than at peace. The physical separation of the classical Greek city-states produced rivalries and wars that contributed much to their decay. The Byzantine Empire (330-1453) experienced several religious schisms, and it was rare for the Greeks to unite even during their war of independence from the Ottomans (1821-31). The First World War brought about a national schism between supporters of the republic and the monarchy, and many quarrels kept the government from functioning effectively between the wars. During the German conquest in World War II, the Greek resistance fought each other as well as the occupation forces, and in the civil war that followed, the Greeks killed many fellow citizens. Perhaps Holden makes a valid point when he says, "Physical separation has promoted human separatism and uncompromising stones have produced uncompromising minds."[5]

If anything can be said to characterize Greek history, it is constant change. In this century alone Greece has suffered a civil war, two foreign occupations, ten military coups d'etat, a seven-year dictatorship, numerous constitutions, and nearly fifty changes of government. Unfortunately, very few history books in the United States make more than passing reference to Greece's past after its classical times. This means that most U.S. visitors to Greece are completely unaware of many of the important events that shaped the character of its people. Listed below are a few of the more critical events of this century, which may serve as useful discussion points with your Greek acquaintances. Although Greeks generally find it disappointing that outsiders know so little about their country, in general they exhibit a forgiving attitude and are eager to teach those willing to learn.

1. *The Asia Minor Disaster* (1922). Since the fall of Constantinople in 1453, the Greeks have kept alive the *Megali Idea* (Great Idea) to bring under Greek rule all the lands of the former Byzantine Empire. This included the lands of Asia Minor, where Greeks had been living since antiquity, when they colonized the western coast of what is now the country of Turkey. Under the leadership of the greatest hero of modern Greece, Eleftherios Venizelos, it seemed that this idea might become reality. Following the Balkan wars of 1912-13, Greece more than doubled in size with the acquisition of the territories of Epirus and Macedonia in the north, and after the First World War it was given permission by the Allies to occupy the Asia Minor city Smyrna (with more Greek inhabitants than Athens) and its surrounding area. However, the Greek army launched an ill-advised offensive into the interior of Turkey and met a swift and devastating end at the hands of the Turks, led by Mustafa Kemal, who later became known as Atatürk, the founder of modern Turkey. As Turkish troops took their revenge on the Greek population in Asia Minor, killing 30,000 civilians in Smyrna, tens of thousands of refugees fled to Greece. A negotiated settlement forced Greece to give up its claim to land in Asia Minor and accept an exchange of populations with Turkey. Practically all Greek Orthodox Christians in the eastern littoral of the Aegean, the Sea of Marmara, and the shores of the Black Sea were to be sent to Greece, and nearly all the Muslims in Greece were to be moved to Turkey.

This resulted in the uprooting of one and a half million Orthodox Christians and approximately 400,000 Muslims. Greece, a country of only six million, was ill equipped to handle this influx of panic-stricken and destitute refugees, some of whom spoke only Turkish. Although many were highly educated, most came only with what they could carry. The Asia Minor disaster has come to be known simply as the *Catastrophe*. It was many decades before the refugees were brought into the mainstream of society, but they quickly contributed to a greater, richer, and more culturally sophisticated Greece. Because of these enforced exchanges, Greece is one of the most homogenous states within Europe and the Balkans.

2. *German Occupation* (1941-44). One of the proudest moments in Greek history is the morning of 28 October 1940, when the Greek dictator Metaxas rejected out of hand the ultimatum delivered to him by Mussolini that he cede control over Greek territory. Within hours Italian forces crossed the Greek-Albanian frontier and Greece was at war. Driven by a great sense of national pride, the Greeks stood up to the bullying of the Italians and drove them back into Albanian territory within days, despite the superiority of the invading forces. The Greek campaign stalled in the face of severe winter weather while trying to free the Greek-speaking parts of Albania. Faced with the need to secure his Balkan flank in advance of the invasion of the Soviet Union, Hitler sent his forces to invade Greece in the spring of 1941, overcoming the poorly equipped Greek army. The resulting tripartite occupation (German, Italian, and Bulgarian) was particularly harsh. Over 67,000 Greek Jews, nearly 90 percent of the total Jewish population, lost their lives during the Axis occupation,[6] the country's agricultural resources were plundered, industry was demolished, communication and transportion networks were in ruins, and over 1,500 villages were destroyed, leaving 700,000 Greeks homeless. In the winter of 1941-42 over 100,000 Athenians died of starvation. In all,

over 8 percent of the population perished. The only other Allied power that had suffered more during the war was the Soviet Union. But even during their struggle for daily survival, the Greeks stubbornly defied the Germans, sometimes through individual acts of sabotage but mostly through organized resistance groups. The accomplishments of these resistance groups contributed much to the Allied cause. The need for Hitler to keep so many of his troops deployed in Greece weakened his forces elsewhere, especially those invading Russia.

3. *Civil War* (1945-49). Although the Greeks have always fought with one another, perhaps no single period has proved as divisive as the civil war that followed the German occupation of World War II. During the war, several resistance groups had sprung up, eventually dividing into a conservative nationalist group and a stronger Communist-led group, who fought each other as well as the Germans. When the Germans withdrew in 1944, the struggle for control of the country turned into a full-scale civil war. With a great deal of help from the British and the Americans (in the way of armaments), the Communist forces were finally defeated in 1949, with many of the retreating forces taking refuge in Yugoslavia and other countries with Communist governments. On top of the damage from the German occupation, another 80,000 were killed and 700,000 left homeless. It was a brutal war in which numerous atrocities were committed by both sides, and it divided villages, neighbors, and even families. The wounds were so deep that it was twenty-five years before the Communist Party was legalized in Greece, and only in the early 1980s were the Communist fighters who fled the country allowed to return to their native land.

4. *Rule by Military Junta* (1967-74). A group of ultra right-wing junior officers in the Greek army, led by Colonel Papadopoulos, mounted a coup against the elected Greek government on 21 April 1967. This military junta was in power for the next seven years, during which time it impris-

oned or exiled most of its political opponents. The regime's cruel actions were the subject of many rhetorical condemnations abroad, but there were few Western powers who took much action against it. The U.S. administration, which was seen by many Greeks as having been instrumental in installing the dictatorship in the first place, looked upon the regime as a point of stability in a volatile region, and it continued American aid to Greece. One of the most bitterly remembered events during the period of the junta was the brutal suppression of a student uprising that culminated in the occupation of the Athens Polytechnic. The troops and police, supported by tanks, put an end to the occupation on 17 November 1973. Several streets in Greece and a well-known terrorist group have been named after this infamous date. The perception of U.S. support for the junta continues to be a source of anti-American feeling for many Greeks.

5. *Turkish Intervention in Cyprus* (1974). After the fall of the Ottoman Empire, the island of Cyprus became a British colony, gaining its independence in 1960 after a bitter armed struggle. At that time, the occupants of the island, which was 80 percent Greek-speaking Orthodox Christians and 20 percent Turkish-speaking Muslims, lived in relative peace in integrated communities. Hostilities in 1963 led to the establishment of Turkish-Cypriot enclaves scattered throughout the island. Tensions remained high over the next decade, with many in Greece and Cyprus calling for *enosis*, or union, with the Greek state, an action strongly opposed by the Turkish Cypriots and by Turkey, whose mainland lies only eighty kilometers to the north of the island. In 1974, the military regime in Athens helped launch a coup against the Cyprus government in order to force enosis, and Turkey responded by sending troops to the northern part of the island. Greek Cypriots living in the north fled their homes, leaving behind all their possessions. Most of the Turkish Cypriots living in the south also left their homes for the north, and the island was partitioned, with the two sides

separated by United Nations peacekeeping forces. During the fighting, civilians on both sides were killed or taken prisoner, and many are still missing. The island has remained divided since 1974, although only the Republic of Cyprus, consisting almost entirely of Greek Cypriots, is internationally recognized. The situation has strained Greek and Turkish relations since that time, more than once bringing the two countries to the brink of war. Greeks believe that the United States should do more to force Turkey to withdraw its troops from Cyprus, and the perceived U.S. support for Turkey (an important NATO ally) is a sore point for many in both Cyprus and Greece.

6. *The Macedonian Question* (1990s). When the various regions of former Yugoslavia broke off into independent states after the collapse of the Soviet Union, none of them had a more complex mixture of ethnic groups than Macedonia, which consists of Albanians, Serbs, Gypsies, Greeks, Turks, and Vlachs. The area comprising the new state of Macedonia has historically been claimed by Greece, Albania, Bulgaria, and Serbia. The Macedonians took as the design for their flag the royal symbol from the time of Philip (father of Alexander the Great) that was found in recent excavations in Vergina in the Macedonian province of Greece. The Greeks strenuously object to both the name of the new country and its use of a Greek symbol. They enforced an economic blockade of Macedonia (lifted in 1995), and they refrain from calling it by that name, using instead the name of its capital city, Skopje. They have also tried in vain to prevent international recognition of Macedonia. The Greeks greatly fear that Macedonia will be taken over by Bulgaria, which desperately wants an outlet to the Aegean and might attempt to form a greater Bulgaria that would include the territories of northern Greece that are called "Aegean Macedonia" by the Bulgarians. The country of Macedonia is very poor and politically unstable, and if it collapses, there would be trouble in the region that could bring Greece into war with its Balkan

neighbors and with Turkey. The United States is perceived by the Greeks as favoring the Muslim over the Christian populations of the Balkans, and its decision to recognize Macedonia as an independent state angered many Greeks.

These critical events represent only a brief glimpse of the extremely complex history that Greeks face as the future moves up on them from behind. However, they serve as defining moments in recent Greek history and shape many current Greek attitudes. In addition, the perceived role of the United States in many of these events affects how Greeks respond to visitors from this country. Although Greeks do not expect the outsider to possess a detailed understanding of their recent history, they are eager to share their views on these issues, and familiarity with the milestones described above will increase greatly the opportunities for meaningful dialogue.

Greek Identity

Isocrates, in the fourth century B.C., stated that a Greek is any person educated as a Greek. By education he was referring to more than formal education; he meant someone who had incorporated Greek values and learned all the Greek ways. Outwardly at least, Greeks have a very strong sense of themselves, a sense that is connected to language, religion, culture, and historical continuity.

While there have been numerous attempts since the time of Isocrates to link territory, religion, and language with the notion of "Greekness," Greek identity has never been a simple issue. It cannot be linked solely with language, as there were many Greeks living in Asia Minor or along the Black Sea coast until 1922 who spoke only Turkish, and until the beginning of this century there were pockets of Greeks even in the Peloponnese who spoke Albanian or Slavic as their first language.[7] Neither can it be connected directly with ethnicity, since people from many lands, including Albanians, Slavs,

Bulgarians, Turks, and Italians have been absorbed into Greek culture. Greek identity is further complicated by other factors, including the Ottoman period. For example, it is easy to see how the four hundred years of Ottoman rule over Greek lands and people influenced its culture—in folklore, vernacular speech, music, cuisine, dress, attitudes, and even some social customs. Similar influence must have resulted from earlier Roman and Frankish occupations, as well as from contacts with the peoples of Alexander's conquests. Yet most Greeks either ignore or deny this influence, preferring to focus on how Greeks have influenced others. There are two primary factors that have had a significant impact on how Greeks define themselves.

First, identity as a Greek has never been linked solely with the borders of the country. The concept of Greece as a nation-state first came about in 1831, following its war of independence from the Ottomans. Throughout the Ottoman occupation, Greece had no independent political existence, and during the thousand years of the Byzantine era, the Orthodox Church ruled an empire, not a nation-state. The Balkan Peninsula that today is called Greece was viewed by the rulers in Constantinople as an impoverished province, and not a great deal of importance was attached to its past cultural achievements. Under Roman rule, the Greek peninsula was an obscure fief of the empire with the name *Graecia*, from which is taken the name by which Westerners still call the country. After the conquests of Alexander the Great, the primary centers of Hellenism moved to cities like Alexandria and Antioch. Ancient Greece had no frontiers. It was a region that varied from century to century and never coincided with the state of modern Greece. The important political entities were city-states, united by a common language and culture but just as often fighting against each other as cooperating. Thus, for most of the past 3,000 years, Greeks have thought of themselves as "Greeks" without the existence of an intact and clearly defined territorial entity called "Greece."[8]

Second, Greece is situated between Eastern and Western forces that have been in opposition for millennia. An important aspect of Greek identity involves the extent to which it can be considered an Eastern or a Western country. Today, when Greeks prepare to go abroad to Germany, England, or France, many say, "We are going to Europe." This may seem odd, given that Greece is a full member of the European Union, and most people think of Greece as the cradle of Western civilization. It is ironic that while the West looks to Greece for the source of its own identity, for most of its history the sights of Greece have been turned toward the East. In ancient times, Alexander the Great turned his back on what he considered a barbarian West and spread Hellenism to the East as far as India. When Constantine established his religious headquarters, it was the growing town of Byzantium that he chose, not the small village of Athens, with its few houses spread beneath a forgotten Acropolis. The Orthodox Church, which was the primary force behind Greek identity for nearly 1,500 years, has always maintained a strongly anti-Western stance.[9] Early Christianity was an Eastern religion, and its adoption by the Greeks preserved its mystical elements while the Roman Church was moving toward greater concern with hierarchy and authority. As late as the 1920s, when Greece sought to expand its borders, it was for parts of Asia Minor that it fought.

Until recent times, the West has been seen as more of a threat than a source of inspiration and support. The split in the Christian church between its Eastern and Western sectors in 1054 left the Orthodox with a strong animosity toward cultural and political structures that emanated from the Roman Catholic Church. The Crusades, during the twelfth and thirteenth centuries, resulted in the Western conquest of Constantinople and were seen as assaults on the Byzantine Empire as much as they were efforts to free the Holy Land. In fact, in the thirteenth century the Frankish occupation of most of what constitutes modern Greece left wounds that were at the time as deep as those resulting from the Ottoman occupation. When Rome refused to aid the Byzantines in the siege of Constantinople by the Ottomans in 1453, it resulted in the city's fall and the end of the Byzantine Empire. This failure to provide assistance has never been forgotten by the Greeks.

Today, perhaps for the first time since Homer's Odysseus sailed westward after the Trojan War, the eyes of Greece are turning to the West. Economically, socially, and culturally Greece is rapidly becoming more Western in its orientation. This process started with the intervention of Britain and France during Greece's war for independence, resulting in a Western-style government that was suddenly thrust upon a more traditional culture. Continued dependence on Britain and the United States for military and economic aid and Greece's decision to enter the European Union profoundly affected its identity as a Western country. Perhaps just as important, most of the six million tourists who visit Greece each year come from the United States, Canada, and European countries. In addition, almost all of the television programming comes from these same sources. Together, these forces have helped transform Greece into a modern consumer society in which the desires and preferences of its people are increasingly identical with those of other European countries.

The ties that have developed with Europe in the past two decades do not mean, however, that all Greeks desire to become a part of Western Europe. There is still a substantial minority that objects to strengthening ties with the West, and there are few in Greece who feel enthusiastic about being part of a community in which they are outsiders and underdogs. Neither is the feeling of most European Union member nations very positive toward Greece. Not only have large sums of money been poured into Greece with no apparent improvement in the long-term economic situation of the country, but Greece is continuously in dispute with the other members over relations with Macedonia and Turkey. It has been said that if the European Union had a procedure to expel members, Greece would be the first to go.

Although most Greeks might see it differently, there are aspects of its history and current situation that point to stronger ties with the Balkans than to either Western Europe or the Near East. Its location is an extension of the Balkan Peninsula, its geography is similar to its northern neighbors, it was under the same Ottoman rule and inherited many of the same problems, and it fought alongside Serbia and Bulgaria against the Ottomans in the Balkan wars earlier in this century. Many economists argue that Greece should look to the Balkans for its economic future. The countries to its north not only provide a ready market for many of its goods and services, but Greece has ports through which it can ship goods produced in the Balkan countries for the growing markets of the Middle East and North Africa. James Pettifer has argued that if Greece defined itself more clearly as a Balkan nation, it could play the role of the regional superpower rather than the poor kid on the block that it will likely continue to play in Europe. In this case, there might be more opportunity to reaffirm many features of traditional Greek life that are in danger of being lost to the "technocratic and conformist" culture of the Western world.[10]

In reality, Greece is neither Eastern, Western, nor Balkan. It is a point where East and West meet in a unique way, a small spot on the map that has left an indelible mark on almost the entire world. Some might say that Greece is not really a place at all, in the normal sense of the word, but rather a seesaw in permanent motion. An important symbol of Greece for the past sixteen centuries has been the double-headed eagle, chosen by officials during the early years of the Eastern Roman Empire of Byzantium. This symbol was selected to represent the two directions that the new empire must face simultaneously, and indeed Greeks have been compelled to look both East and West at the same time during most of their history. The eagle, however, is not a symbol of a static entity but rather the representation of a force that is constantly in flux. Certainly Greece has seen its share of action from many directions, as forces of both East and West have advanced toward, fought over, suffered upon, and retreated from its lands.

The Greek Diaspora

From ancient times the Greeks have turned their sights beyond their *patrida* (fatherland). As early as the fifth century B.C., according to Thucydides, Greek communities were scattered throughout the Mediterranean. It was no accident that the oracle of Delphi advised the Greeks to go forth and colonize other lands. The most famous of Greek travelers, Homer's Odysseus, spent ten years wandering distant lands after the Trojan War, and his very name has become synonymous with long journeys. The city-states of ancient Greece established colonies in almost every part of their known world. Later, Alexander of Macedonia through his conquests spread Hellenic culture both east to Asia and south to Egypt. One of the lesser-known legacies of Alexander's excursions is the Greeks who stayed in northern India, ruling there for twenty generations. For much of its history, identity as a Greek was determined not by geography but by one's association with the Hellenic culture. During Byzantine times, the very heart of the Greek world was moved to Asia Minor, away from the ancient centers of Hellenic civilization. This resulted in adherence to the Orthodox Christian religion, which became the primary defining characteristic of "Greekness." Under Ottoman rule Greek merchants established a mercantile empire in the eastern Mediterranean, the Balkans, North Africa, and as far away as India.

The tendency to leave Greece for distant lands has continued in the last two centuries. Several great waves of emigration have deposited large numbers of Greeks in the United

States, Canada, Australia, England, and Germany, as well as significant numbers in various African and South American countries. These immigrants have helped build the countries to which they have immigrated, and they have brought changes to them as well. Cities such as Chicago and Melbourne have larger Greek populations than any city in Greece itself except for Athens and Thessaloniki. In some cases, the Greek populations of these countries are in the third and fourth generations, and yet they still identify strongly with their Greek heritage if not with their patrida. Altogether, there are approximately four million people who speak Greek, or think of themselves as Greek, scattered around the world. Given that the population of Greece is only ten million, the Greeks who live outside the country constitute a significant expansion of its borders, psychologically and economically.

The Greek diaspora is the result of the two primary characteristics of the Greek landscape, the harsh and divisive mountainous terrain and the lengthy coastline. The mountains have fragmented Greece and discouraged internal communications, and the lack of large fertile plains and valleys combined with the lack of natural resources has limited the degree to which Greece could adequately support its own population. At the same time, the sea has provided a natural outlet for overseas trade. As Holden says: "Poverty uproots the Greeks and the sea carries them away."[11]

The Greek diaspora has had both a positive and a negative effect on the country. From their travels to faraway places, the ancient voyagers brought back with them many ideas and customs that enriched Greek philosophy, literature, and the overall quality of Greek life. Their curiosity translated into creativity, allowing the Greeks to contribute to the world in ways that far exceeded their numbers. Some of the best-known Greeks of this century have come from the diaspora, including the poets Seferis and Cavafy and the business tycoon Onassis. In addition, it has affected the Greek sense of national identity, as so many of its citizens find themselves in what they refer to as *xenitia*, or exile. Fortunately, the exile is usually self-imposed and rarely results in a loss of identity as a Greek. In fact, it appears that a sense of national identity remains with almost all individuals of Greek descent no matter how long they live in a foreign land. This tenacious sense of Greekness has produced a strong political lobby in the United States and elsewhere, often bringing Greece a greater proportion of military and economic aid than its size and strategic importance would otherwise favor. Finally, the diaspora has channeled a significant inflow of funds from abroad as workers send money home to families and as they return to Greece to set up businesses or retire. These remittances are a significant source of income for the country, helping to account for Greece's relatively high standard of living and low poverty rate.

On the other hand, in modern times the diaspora has imposed both a physical and a psychological burden on the Greek people and the Greek nation. This is reflected in many songs of exile in which mothers cry out for their sons who are far away. One popular song begins with "Heavy are the foreign lands" (*Varia ine ta ksena*), a reference to the psychological difficulties experienced by the immigrant. The effects of the diaspora go far beyond the feelings of the person living outside of Greece, however. As for many "Third World" countries, the exodus of so many of its best minds has drained Greece of much-needed talent and initiative, thereby harming its own economic and social development. It has also brought some confusion to Greece's national self-image. Those living outside have usually become accustomed to a better standard of living, greater efficiency, and the availability of better services than their Greek counterparts, and when they return to their country they don't hesitate to openly criticize what they find. This contributes to the victim mentality that is a natural by-product of the many calamities suffered by the Greek people· (although this mentality is reflected more in the style of discourse and the topics of discussion than in low self-esteem). Finally, the diaspora has fueled the pace for rapid social change within Greece as immigrants return from abroad, bringing with them new values and greater material aspirations.

One unfortunate by-product of the Greek diaspora is the nostalgic and usually romantic image of the homeland maintained by those who have spent their lives outside the country. When Greeks return to their country after many years abroad, they are often disappointed by the many changes they see, and they have a difficult time adjusting to the place they now call home. This can lead not only to misunderstandings about how Greeks feel toward various political situations, but also to unrealistic views of events that take place in Greece during times of crisis.[12]

In one of my Greek language lessons, my teacher expressed her surprise when I already knew the meaning of the word "diaspora." I told her that we use it in English to refer to the Jews and the great dispersal of their people that took place after the fall of Jerusalem. After reminding me that the word is of Greek origin, she said: "Well, after the Jews, we are next." Only later did I realize how central the experience of friends, family, or oneself living outside the patrida has been to the historical experience of Greek people of all ages. It is reflected in their music, their literature, and their poetry. No attempt to enter the world of modern Greeks would advance far without an appreciation of the influence of the diaspora on their self-image and worldview.

The Future

A strong sense of their past assures the Greek people that they hold a special place in the world and have an important contribution to make to humanity. Perhaps because they are small in number and surrounded by Slav, Turkish, and Arab neighbors, they often feel like a lonely outpost perched on the southeastern edge of Western culture, the essence of which sprang from their own glorious past. One Greek told me: "We gave light to the world, and we still hold the candle." Some Greeks believe that Western consumerism and pop culture are a distortion of original Greek ideals, and many fear that the candle they hold is in danger of being snuffed out by the very culture they helped to create. Greece has experienced a myriad of difficult struggles in its past, many of which threatened its very existence. That it has endured is a testament to the strength, stamina, and intelligence of its people. The Greeks themselves tend to be pessimistic about their future, but as my friend so clearly demonstrated with the glasses of ouzo, their survival may lie in their ability to look forward to the past, from where their power most certainly flows.

---

[1] Nikos Kazantzakis, *Journey to the Morea* (New York: Simon and Schuster, 1965), 7.

[2] Only one-sixth of Greece's surface is level enough to be cultivated. Two-thirds of Greece is mountainous or too rocky for farming. The lowlands are divided by the heights of the mountains into over 6,000 separate communities. However, no place in Greece is more than 100 kilometers (60 miles) from the sea.

[3] The services sector (transportation, communication, trade, banking, public administration, defense) is 55 percent of GNP. The agricultural sector (grains, fruits, vegetables, wine, tobacco, cotton, livestock, dairy products) employs 28 percent of the labor force but is only 14 percent of GNP, and industry (processed foods, textiles, metals, chemicals, cement, glass) is 31 percent of GNP.

[4] Holden, *Greece without Columns*, 32.

[5] Ibid., 58.

[6] Most of the Greek Jews lived in the northern city of Thessaloniki, where they formed 50 percent of the population when the city was incorporated into the Greek kingdom in 1912. These Sephardic Jews were the descendants of the Jews expelled from Spain in 1492, who had been offered refuge in the Ottoman Empire. Elsewhere in Greece, there were small communities of "Romaniot" Jews whose roots in Greece went back to antiquity.

See Richard Clogg, A Concise History of Greece (Cambridge: Cambridge University Press, 1992), 131.

[7] Laurie Kain Hart, Time, Religion, and Social Experience in Rural Greece (Lanham, MD: Rowman and Littlefield Publishers, 1992).

[8] Even when Greece became a nation-state in 1831, its territory was only a fraction of what it is today. Initially, the new state comprised a very small area, consisting primarily of what we know today as central Greece and the Peloponnese. The majority of its current territory was acquired during the twentieth century. Much of its northern lands were gained following the Balkan wars of 1912-13, when Crete (its largest island) became part of Greece, along with Macedonia and the Aegean islands. After the First World War, Greece gained Thrace, both the western section that is part of Greece today and the eastern section that included Constantinople. However, it was forced to return the latter territory to Turkey following its defeat in the Greco-Turkish war that ended in 1923. More recent was the acquisition of the Dodecanese islands from Italy as part of the peace settlement following the Second World War. As late as 1974, when Greek-led forces in Cyprus tried to unite the island with Greece, there existed the possibility of expanding the size of the country. Today there is still concern within Greece about its territorial integrity, as threats are perceived from Turkey in eastern Thrace and the Aegean and from the former Yugoslavian state of Macedonia in the north.

[9] In fact, there was a deliberate attempt by the early Byzantine Church to stamp out those elements of Greek heritage that were considered most Western, particularly the pagan temples, gods, and classical traditions such as the Olympic games. Even the Athens academies were closed in the name of Christian cleansing.

[10] James Pettifer, The Greeks: The Land and the People since the War (New York: Viking Penguin, 1993), 237.

[11] Holden, Greece without Columns, 60.

[12] Nicholas Gage provides a vivid example of immigrants being out of touch with events in Greece in his book Eleni (New York: Random House, 1983). This story takes place during the Greek civil war and chronicles the lives of a family where the husband was away, working in the United States during the period of turmoil that accompanied the struggle between Communist and Nationalist forces for control of Greece. From his faraway vantage

point, he could not understand the dangers of war that his family faced, and he failed to listen to their pleas for his assistance until it was too late. It should be noted that Gage's book presents what many consider to be a biased view of the role of the Communists in the events of the civil war. Although his mother's death by the *andartes* (guerrilla fighters) is not disputed, many in Greece have criticized his failure to acknowledge the atrocities committed by the Nationalist forces. In spite of the fact that the book has such strong political connotations for many, I believe Gage does an excellent job of portraying Greek village life during this period.

Cornerstones of Greek Culture

One of the most popular places from which to watch the sunset in Greece is the Temple of Poseidon at Sounion, located approximately seventy kilometers (by road) from Athens on the tip of the Attica peninsula. By the time you make the trip along the coast to Sounion, it is likely that you will have already visited the Parthenon, and you may also have journeyed across the Saronic Gulf to the island of Aegina, where a temple is dedicated to Aphaia, a little-known goddess. What the guidebook may fail to tell you is that these three temples form an isosceles triangle, and at Sounion you are standing equidistant from both the Parthenon and the Temple of Aphaia. This triangle is an interesting mathematical phenomenon, and it is one of several geometric relationships that exist among the ancient temples and religious sites in Greece. Some have argued that such relationships express the symmetry of ancient Greek thought.[1]

In a corresponding manner, the basis of social order and culture in Greece today is reflected in a triangular pattern, the cornerstones of which are village, family, and religion. The three components of this system are connected in an integral manner with one another, and together they provide the context within which interpersonal relations in Greece are deeply embedded. While the lines that join them do not have a mathematical relationship and are less precise than those that link the ancient temples of Athena, Poseidon, and Aphaia, it is within the boundaries defined by these elements that individuals function and society operates.

It is not a simple task, unfortunately, to clarify meaningfully the significance of village culture, family life, and religious influence. Greek thought and action are psychologically and socially bound to a traditional culture that influences their lives in a myriad of ways. At first glance, it might seem that Greek society is slowly emerging from a traditional rural to a modern urban way of life. In understanding Greek culture, however, one must suspend the common belief that societies progress in a linear fashion from traditional to modern. Michael Herzfeld, an anthropologist who has conducted several ethnographic studies in Rhodes and Crete, describes modern Greece as "a country that falls disconcertingly between the exotic and the familiar."[2] He warns us that many of the dualities we have created in order to describe other cultures do not fit in the case of Greece. Thus, one finds in the mosaic of Greek culture a merging of the traditional and modern that cannot easily be dissected. Athens is a thoroughly modern city whose people identify strongly with their village community. Two-career families in Greece are quite common, yet the responsibilities of motherhood have not taken a back seat to personal aspirations. Icons are prevalent in the most modern homes and offices, and most drivers keep in their car an image of the saint who protects them while traveling. The naturalness with which Greeks incorporate elements of traditional culture into their modern lives cannot be grasped easily, but it is one of the defining characteristics of Greek social reality.

The Village Community

Historically, Greek life has revolved around village culture, even though Greeks have from preclassical times traveled widely both to satisfy their curiosity and to search for new resources. With seaside ports hugging the twisting coastline and small clusters of stone houses dotting the mostly mountainous countryside, the village has been the characteristic feature of the Greek landscape from time immemorial. While there has always been a general lack of cooperation as well as a great deal of conflict between families in most villages, everyone feels an intense loyalty to the community. Solidarity has often been created through emergencies, common dangers, or religious or community holidays like the village festival. There is usually a community church, and icons or shrines mark the boundaries of the village. Residents born and brought up in the village share a patron saint, common customs, a local identity, and a sense of collective village honor. These bonds within the village create a framework for community social life that would otherwise be inhibited by the inordinately strong Greek sense of family loyalty.

Although the population of Greece today is highly urban, with over half of the people living in the three cities of Athens, Thessaloniki, and Patras, the village continues to play an important role in defining both self-image and social relations. Most city dwellers have their roots in the rural communities, and the dichotomy between village and city is somewhat arbitrary. Migrants to the cities have not lost their sense of membership in the village of their birth or connection with their parents' ancestors. When a villager moves to the city, the corresponding upward mobility and higher status do not lead to a break in social relations with kin remaining in the village. The city dweller sends gifts, stays in touch by telephone, and returns often for special celebrations. In fact, the city dweller feels a sense of almost chauvinistic loyalty to his or her birthplace, and Greeks do not take kindly to unfavorable comparisons with or criticisms of their village.

Correspondingly, villagers feel pride and respect for urban family members and value ties with their city kin, not only for emotional reasons, but also because the relatives in the city may be able to provide valuable assistance in the future. These relatives might help the villagers by arranging medical services for sick family members, by locating items for the farm or house, by obtaining information from government ministries, or by assisting in providing for the education of village kin. When I was teaching in Greece in the early 1980s, there was no need for dormitories at the college, since almost all of the students who came from outside Athens were staying with aunts, cousins, or other close relatives.

The strength of the Greek city dweller's tie with his or her village past is manifested in several ways. First, most Greeks share a lifelong ambition to build a house in the village of their parents (although more often than not this means the village of the husband's parents), perhaps going to live there when they retire. Many of my friends are putting considerable time, money, and energy into restoring their family homeplace or building a new dwelling in their village. Second, when villages celebrate Easter, the village patron saint's day, weddings, funerals, baptisms, or the saints' days of relatives, people return in great numbers to participate in the activities. Church services, singing, dancing, and feasting turn quiet villages of less than a hundred people into vibrant gatherings many times their normal size. Third, Greeks almost always return to their village in order to vote during elections. Most Greeks prefer to keep their voting registration in the village rather than move it to their city of residence, maintaining their ties and status with the village. When elections take place, there is a mass exodus from Athens by boat, car, and plane. Travel outside of Athens is difficult during this time, since there may not be rooms available. Roads are jammed with cars, and buses, boats, and planes are full.

In addition to the pull of the villages on their former

residents and their descendants, village ties also create strong social bonds. The first thing two Greek strangers do in conversation is determine if they come from the same village or province. They might learn that they are remotely related, or at least an acquaintance of a relative. A connection that places one's cousin as an in-law to someone from a nearby village will be enough to ease doubts and smooth the way for good relations. Travel writer William Davenport tells how he once invited the singer in the taverna where he was eating to join him and his friends for a drink. Within two minutes this man and a woman at his table had established that they both came from the same town, and one of her many uncles was godfather to one of the singer's many aunts. He says that while it would be easy to dismiss such an encounter as mere coincidence, this would miss the point that such coincidences are in fact made to happen because the Greeks are constantly seeking to establish and maintain positive links with one another.[3]

In many ways, the modern cities of Greece resemble a collection of urban villages. Most of the population of Athens migrated from the islands and the villages and small towns of the countryside, and most residents of the capital were not born there. It is not unusual for residents of certain *yitonia*, or small neighborhoods, to be from a particular village. In these areas, a great deal of value is placed on sociability. The community becomes a major focus of social organization, the primary arena for communication and social exchange. Unlike the United States, where apartment buildings and neighborhoods tend to be collections of strangers, a great deal of social contact takes place in Greek urban villages. In Athens there are many *syllogi*, or social clubs, composed of individuals from a particular geographical area, and in many cases the importance of the village tie can even become a source of jobs or contacts that lead to employment. It is not uncommon to find that most of the employees of a factory in Athens come from the owner's province.

The Family

The *ikoyenia*, or family, is the basic social unit in Greek society. Loyalty to the family supersedes all competing interests, and much of a person's life is devoted to family obligations and responsibilities. Regardless of region, class, or location, the family does not lose its central importance. The people of Greece have been through difficult times, and the family unit has been the only stable entity in which trust could be placed. James Pettifer refers to the family as the "domestic fortress," and sees it as "the only reliable source of fundamental security against an inimical world."[4]

Throughout their lives Greeks maintain a close relationship with the family, which provides both economic and emotional security and, simultaneously, places many demands on its members. Obligations to the family are taken seriously, and the needs of the family take precedence over one's own needs, wishes, and interests. Everyone shares in the failures and triumphs, difficulties and successes of fellow family members in a way that seems extreme to many Western visitors.

Traditionally, roles and responsibilities in the family have been clearly defined, sometimes even written into law. Until 1983, when a new family law was passed, the Greek Civil Code outlined the rights and responsibilities of husband and wife. Under this code, a married woman was subject to her husband in all matters; the husband, for instance, could legally administer the woman's property or forbid her to work. The 1983 family law officially implemented equality between the sexes, replacing the husband's legal right to be family head with joint decision making. Civil marriage was officially recognized for the first time in 1982, prior to which only marriages performed by the Orthodox Church were sanctioned. Divorce by mutual consent also became possible. Until this time, adultery was a criminal offense and people could serve jail sentences if convicted.

In reading the description of Greek family life which follows, the Westerner is likely to view the values and behaviors of Greek society as underdeveloped and reflecting a dominant male orientation. Those in Western countries who have struggled for many years to help change the subservient position of women and to promote more influence of the feminine perspective in business and politics may recoil in response to the strictly defined role of women in Greece. We may wonder why more Greek women are not engaged in a struggle for their rights and a greater role in political decisions. It is easy to see Greece as a place where the woman slaves away at home while the men roam or sit around the kafenion discussing politics and sports and playing *tavli* (backgammon).

The overall picture is more complex, however, and it is important to refrain from judging the position of women from a Western perspective. It is helpful to differentiate between the *form* of the behavior and its *function* in the context of Greek culture. In Greece, where seemingly contradictory positions can exist side by side, neither sex is viewed as having more power than the other, or of playing a more important role in society than the other. Rather, a delicate balance exists between the sexes in Greece, and the sharp distinction between the roles of men and women is seen by most Greeks as both natural and necessary.

The marriage relationship

In traditional rural culture, men and women were believed to have different natures, with each sex having its own set of duties and responsibilities. There was a fairly strict division of labor, with the activities of one sex complementing those of the other. Generally, males felt incompetent or ashamed to do the tasks of women, and many women felt likewise about the jobs of men. Men were the primary breadwinners, while women took responsibility for homemaking, including the preparation of food and keeping the house orderly and clean. A woman's first duty was to have children and care for them properly. Overall, hers was a nurturing role.[5]

Although there are many signs of change, husbands and wives in Greece still inhabit separate worlds. Some of the men in today's younger generation may have different attitudes, but few of my male friends in Greece will go near the kitchen unless absolutely necessary, and they share almost none of the housework and little of the child care. When asked to contribute to such chores, you might hear the man ask with an air of amazement: *Thelis na mou foresis foustania?* or "Do you want me to wear a dress?" Today's working woman may have a maid who helps with household chores, but she still takes overall responsibility for the work. For most couples, marriage is a cooperative effort or a working arrangement based on the complementary roles of husband and wife and their relationship of mutual dependence.

The attitude of my male friends became apparent to me one Saturday morning when I went with my neighbor to buy some materials to build a screen door for my veranda in order to keep out the mosquitoes during the approaching summer months. We left the house around 10:00 A.M., and I told my wife I would be back in less than an hour, since the shop we were going to was nearby. On the way my neighbor asked if I would mind accompanying him to the cemetery so he could lay flowers on the grave of his parents. As it turned out, the cemetery was across town nearly an hour away. I was not in a particular hurry, so I didn't mind. When we returned to the store to buy the materials it was closed, so we had to go to a different part of town to find another store. On the way home we stopped to see a friend of his, who invited us for a sandwich and beer. I tried to say politely that I needed to go home, but it was impossible to refuse the hospitality. An hour later we finally started home, the time now being midafternoon. When I said to my neighbor that my wife would be worried about me for being gone so long, he told me: *Min tous mathenis na se perimenoun*, or "Don't let them become accustomed to expecting you back at a certain time" (literally, "Don't teach them to wait for you"). He then explained that if your wife expects you to return at a certain time, then she will start to worry if you are later than you indicated. In this case you will have lost your freedom.

Most of the power of Greek women remains out of public display.[6] In the home the mother is the key figure, with responsibility for all that goes on within it, and in this context she exercises control of the most basic elements of society, including the finances of the home, attitudes of the children, and decisions made by the husbands. Some have gone so far as to describe Greece as a matriarchal society, where men receive most of the public credit but have little real influence. Although this statement probably represents an extreme view, there are many ways in which women exert power over men. Renee B. Hirschon describes it this way:

> For their part, women take pride in their ability to manage their husbands. They must develop special diplomatic skills in dealing with the men of their families, first with fathers and brothers, and later with their husbands and sons. This ability to influence and manipulate people, especially husbands, women refer to as their "manner." "I have my way," a woman says. But in the presence of men women rarely refer to it since the skill itself is that of persuading a man to adopt a point of view or course of action while allowing him to believe that the initiative is his. Even among women this topic is not discussed and any attempt to elicit what constitutes the "manner" or "way" fails to gain any clear explanation.[7]

While in general Greeks are affectionate toward one another within the family, the husband-wife relationship is characterized by less intimacy than Westerners would find desirable. In the United States, we have become accustomed to the notion that a successful marriage is built on closeness, satisfying sex, and a sharing of common interests. While such relationships certainly exist in Greece, especially among the younger generation, in general this image is not held up as the ideal of marriage. Although it is no longer common, for hundreds of years marriages were arranged according to economic and status concerns of the bride's and groom's parents rather than on mutual attraction between the couple. Today's young people are more free to chose their own partners, but social and economic concerns are just as important as personal or sexual attraction.

There are differences, of course, between urban and rural areas and between the highly educated and those with less formal education; nevertheless, a successful and happy marriage is still seen by many Greeks as dependent on mutual understanding, display of good personal character, and mutual concessions rather than on love. Emotions are channeled into the parent-child relationship.[8] When a woman has worries or concerns, she discusses them with other women more often than with her husband. For many Greek marriages, this is especially true from the middle years of their lives, when erotic love may no longer play a major role in binding husband and wife. The emotion they share is that of *synennoisis*, a common understanding and ability to come to agreements. In old age the spouse is sometimes described as a *syntrophos*, a companion or comrade, who provides company against loneliness. At this stage of life, whether or not there is a sharing of interests or even much personal conversation, the company they provide to each other is very meaningful.[9]

The place of children

As it was in traditional rural culture, motherhood is still highly valued, and a mother represents all the positive aspects of home. The relationship of a mother with her children is often emotionally more important to her than the relationship with her husband. A mother sacrifices a great deal for her children, and the children develop a strong attachment to their mother. No one who has seen the movie *Never on Sunday* will forget the scene when Homer, the American who wanted to be the savior of Greece, tells one of the men in the taverna that the root of his (the other man's) problems is that he hated his mother. The reaction Homer received from his unsolicited psychoanalysis (including the resulting black eye that the man in the taverna gave him) is an appropriate Greek response to the ultimate insult. Harry C. Triandis reports that once in an opening speech to the Greek parliament, a new MP (minister of parliament), while looking at the spectator's gallery where his proud mother was seated, began his remarks with the words: "Mother, Your Majesty, Distinguished Members of the House, Ladies and Gentlemen."[10]

The period of Ottoman rule is condemned in Greece for many reasons, but the most negative feelings about this time relate to the *pedomazoma*, literally "child gathering," that took place until the end of the seventeenth century. This was a levy, imposed at irregular intervals, in which Greeks were required to give their best-looking and most intelligent sons to become elite soldiers or bureaucrats. These children were required to convert to Islam, and they spent their lives in service to the Ottoman state. More recently, an incident involving children occurred at the end of the civil war in the late 1940s, when the retreating Communist forces took children (both boys and girls) from certain villages in the north over the border into Albania and other Soviet-bloc countries.[11] This taking of children had such an emotional impact on the public that for twenty-five years its occurrence was used by political powers to help prevent the Communist Party from gaining political recognition or even acknowledgment of its role during resistance to the German occupation, despite the fact that a large percentage of Greeks had supported the Communists during the civil war. Children are so important to Greeks that any perceived attack on their connection to the family engenders negative feelings that do not disappear easily.

While it is not so widespread now, traditionally there was a strong preference for sons over daughters. Ethnographer

Irvin T. Sanders, who studied rural parts of Greece in the early 1960s, reported that when asked how many children he has, a man might reply, "Two sons and, begging your pardon, one daughter." Or he may have said, "Two children and one girl." In some villages the father would use a poetic touch in answering, "Two sons and one guest," thus implying that the daughter's permanent home is that of her husband.[12] This traditional preference for sons had much to do with the former need to provide a *prika*, or dowry, for daughters, who thus became a heavy financial burden. Hirschon, in her work in an Athens community, said that daughters are sometimes referred to as *grammatia*, which is literally "promissory notes" or "mortgages."[13]

Today the dowry system does not officially exist, and most parents no longer view daughters as economic liabilities. In cases where our friends have both sons and daughters, there seems to be more equal treatment. Much of the overprotectiveness, for instance, traditionally bestowed on the son and the pressure for him to succeed, are now shared by daughters. In spite of the changing situation in contemporary Athens, one must keep in mind that most of the men currently comprising the professional class were raised in an environment where they were given special treatment because they were sons, and it takes time for old habits to change.

The Greek approach to discipline of children is sometimes difficult for the Westerner to understand. The ability to hold one's own in conversation is a skill that is learned early and cultivated throughout childhood to a much larger extent than it is in the United States. At social and cultural events such as concerts, for instance, children are often allowed to have almost free run of the place, much to the consternation of foreigners, who more often expect children to be either kept away from the event or kept under control. In fact, the very notion of control takes on a different meaning in the Greek context, beginning at an early age. Similar to children in the United States, Greek youngsters learn early that the parent will often forget a command entirely if it is ignored, but with Greeks this approach to authority becomes more ingrained and is carried over into adult life, where so many rules and regulations are routinely ignored.

As elsewhere, Greek children learn subtle survival skills, such as how to manipulate the world around them to their own advantage. *Pisma,* or stubbornness, is not necessarily punished in children, and it may even be grudgingly admired if the child is not excessively recalcitrant. Even taking advantage of a neighbor or someone outside the family may privately meet with approval, especially if it is done by the male child. His parents may secretly brag that their boy is *poniros,* or "clever," knowing that such a skill is essential for survival in the competitive world he will soon enter.[14]

Beyond the nuclear family

When Greeks speak of their ikoyenia, they are not referring only to the mother, father, and children. Elders are important in all families, and in today's urban setting it is the *yiayia,* or grandmother, who often assumes primary responsibility for taking care of the children. She is an enormous source of strength and security for the younger generation, and emotional ties with their grandparents are particularly strong for most children throughout their life. Not only do many households include grandparents, but the larger extended family is an important part of the family structure. For any one person, this group comprises all relatives, both maternal and paternal, to the degree of second cousin, with more distant relatives sometimes included. Relations are usually close between first cousins, and nephews and nieces receive special treatment from their aunts and uncles. Because marriage is a relationship between families, relations with in-laws are also important. A complex network of obligations, debts, and responsibilities exists among members of the extended family—and it follows that Greeks cannot be impartial in awarding jobs or distributing goods. As Dorothy Lee explains, Greeks take care of their own first.[15]

Outside of blood relatives and in-laws, there is another important family member who assumes great responsibility for the welfare of the immediate family—the *koumbaros*, or godfather. Usually, he serves as best man at the wedding of the couple, although he may become koumbaros by standing as godfather to the child after it is born. In either case he is godbrother to the father of the child. The koumbaros becomes a member of the family in an artificially created relationship called spiritual kinship. By entering into this relationship, he is deemed to have entered into the mutual and indissoluble obligations imposed by true blood kinship. Thus he is entitled to the loyalty of his brothers in God, and they are equally entitled to his protection and support. As in a relationship by blood, law restricts marriage between godchildren of the same individual and between the family of the godchild and of the godparent. The relationship is not just between the godparent and the child, but between the two families. Thus, the koumbaros can often act as a mediator when difficulties arise within the family.

Family and society

While it may seem excessive both in its demands and in its degree of support, the contribution of the strong family to the quality of life in Greece cannot be overstated. Its influence leads to social conditions that are the envy of other countries around the world, both industrial and nonindustrial. For example, although crime has doubled in Greece since 1970, the murder rate is still eight times lower than that of the United States. Suicides are rare, the divorce rate is much lower than in most Western countries, and poverty is hard to find. Much of the responsibility for these positive statistics is attributed by Greeks to the strength of the family, since it serves as a strong monitor of the behavior of its members.

The family also serves as a psychological and financial safety net for its members, particularly in times of difficulty. It is responsible for the care of those unable to care for themselves, whether this need is caused by loss of a job, illness, or old age. Unemployment is relatively high, but those affected are able to turn to family for assistance. If at all possible, the elderly, infirm, and orphaned members of the family are kept off public welfare, except in cases where disaster has struck the entire family. It is considered damaging to family honor to allow one of its kin to accept such help. When immediate family is not able to provide support, the extended family members help out.[16]

It might be argued that Greeks do not feel a sense of social responsibility so much as they do a sense of family responsibility. Status and reputation are integral aspects of a family's wealth, and great care is taken to increase it and to preserve it. Nicholas Gage relates the story told to him by a criminal lawyer, who recalled that almost every one of his clients who was involved in a felony was more concerned about his family's reaction to his crime than about the judge's reaction. "The usual family response," he says, "is 'How could you bring such shame on the family?' not, 'Why did you do it?' or 'How have we failed you?'"[17]

As elsewhere, significant changes are taking place in Greece today, and the family is affected more than any other social unit. The cohesive family group that existed in rural areas led to a great deal of sharing and exchange of information and advice, particularly between the female members. Today's urban housewife is more likely to be lonely and frustrated, spending time with her family only in the evening hours, on holidays, and during weekends. Grown daughters in particular are beginning to resent parental restrictions, and when they are able, more of them are seeking a place of their own, although much less frequently than in northern Europe or the United States. Marital expectations are slowly changing to include joint decision making, greater initiative for women, and companionship based on common interests.[18] Friendships formed through work are becoming more important and are replacing some of the functions formerly served by the family.

While it is inevitable that changes will occur as family ties loosen and feminism rises in Greece, the basic sense of family loyalty will probably always be felt much more strongly than in most Western countries. The family has been able to maintain its strength and vitality despite the rapid transformation that Greece has undergone in recent years. Although urbanization, Western consumerism, and other influences are reshaping the outward appearance of family life, the obligations and responsibilities felt by its members are still important, and their influence still pervades society.

Religion

In ancient times the Greeks built their temples on the *acropolis*, or high point of the city, and from almost anywhere the temple was visible. In addition there were numerous shrines and temples throughout the city, so that one was never too far from a religious place. This visibility served to remind the people of higher ideals, to help them remember their own place within the *cosmos*, and to encourage submission to the will of the gods. Although the form of the religion has changed since the classical period of Greek history, and most temples to Zeus, Athena, and Poseidon have been replaced by Christian churches, the sense of always being near the divine has not changed. In villages today the main church is almost always the tallest, largest, and best-constructed building, and it is located, along with the cemetery, in a landscape of natural beauty. For both ancient and contemporary Greeks, religion was closely connected to the natural world and to daily life.[19]

Religion permeates every layer of life in Greece, from the family to politics, from work to recreation. Every building that is put up is blessed by the church, practically every holiday is associated with the church calendar, and every event of the year—from the planting of crops to the first voyage of the village fishing fleet to the first fruits of the harvest—is accompanied by an appropriate religious ceremony. Few Greeks, urban or rural, would initiate anything important without a religious inauguration.[20]

On an individual level, a person's very identity is connected with religion through his or her given name. Almost everyone in Greece is named after a saint or given a Christian name that the church has sanctioned. It is the custom to celebrate one's "nameday" rather than one's birthday, and it is much more a familial and communal affair than a personal one. Instead of receiving presents from others, the celebrant offers sweets to visiting family, friends, and neighbors. If the saint is a major figure, there are special church services that the person will attend. When one observes a nameday, he or she is taking part in an event with all others who share the same name, and in a symbolic way the saint or religious figure is being honored as much as the person with the nameday.

Religious expression is not confined to formal occasions; it pervades daily life. Every family has an icon that protects the members, every person has a saint on whom he or she can call daily. Whenever you enter a church, you will see people lighting candles to send prayers to a saint who might help them with a problem or intercede in a difficult matter. Although those with an illness will visit a doctor, it is likely they will depend to a greater extent on the help of a saint who is thought to be capable of curing the affliction. At shrines and churches dedicated to these saints are hundreds of small, flat silver or gold images of arms, legs, eyes, or bodies of babies or adults that have been offered to the saint to seek a cure. Not only are concerns about sickness brought to these saints, but images are also found of ships, houses, and even animals or cars that need attention. Once I saw an image of a motorcycle hung on an icon, which I took to mean that someone had bought a new bike and was asking for it to be protected.

Greek nationality itself is closely linked with religion. Ninety-seven percent of the people are Greek Orthodox, which is the official religion. Being a member of the Greek Orthodox Church is tantamount to being Greek. Traditionally the Orthodox Christian Church has been closely linked to the state. The concept of separation of church and state is alien to the Greeks, for whom there is a close relationship between Orthodox Christianity and national identity. The constitution declares that "The prevailing religion in Greece is the Eastern Orthodox Church of Christ." Although freedom of religion is guaranteed by the constitution, proselytization by religious groups other than the Orthodox Church is prohibited. Historically, the Orthodox hierarchy has been a strong political force, playing a major role in the revolution for independence and in shaping the resulting Greek state. At the same time, the church itself has been subject to state influence, both in its organization and administration (and some say in its religious tenets). The concept of patrida is so closely associated with religion that the day the Greeks refused to capitulate to Mussolini in 1940 is classified as a religious holiday. In many ways, the modern state is thought of as defender of the faith.[21]

The villager's religion is a special blend of classical Greek paganism and Christianity. Greek culture absorbed early Christianity in such a way as to maintain continuity with its past. Fermor asserts that "The Christian Church was the last great creative achievement of classical Greek culture."[22] While all religions developed from existing practices, the Greek version of Christianity is perhaps more indebted to its predecessor than most people realize. As Sanders said, "The peasant, instead of being made over into some sort of revolutionary Christian image, was able to take early Christianity and make it over into the even earlier Greek image."[23]

While not all Orthodox fathers will accept the notion that Christianity is so indebted to ancient Greek beliefs, most writers agree that to the peasant, the coming of Christianity did not mean an important break with previous practices, beliefs, or even deities. Former deities became saints, and some of the more powerful deities became identified with the most powerful saints, with the same functions and sometimes even the same names. For example, the Greek sun god, Helios, became the prophet Elias, whose shrines are scattered across the hilltops throughout Greece; Theseus, who killed the Minotaur in the labyrinth of King Minos's Palace, became St. George, who slew the evil dragon; Athena Parthenos became the Virgin Mary (in Cyprus, Aphrodite became Mary); Dionysos, the god of wine, became St. Dionysios, who is said to have discovered the grapevine; Demeter, goddess of fertility whose shrine was at Eleusis, had her temple there replaced by a Christian church dedicated to St. Dimitra, to whom women bring offerings in the spring to ensure good crops. Throughout Greece, often situated at bends in the mountain roads, are tiny chapels and shrines dedicated to saints who have rendered some service.[24] Inside each is an icon and an oil lamp that is kept burning whenever possible. In ancient times there were shrines to pagan gods in the same locations. With so many similarities, it is easy to conclude that the new religion was simply grafted onto the old.[25]

Greek religion is so full of feast days and ceremonies, weaving through the year a "continuous thread of the spiritual and supernatural,"[26] that anyone who tried to observe all of them would spend most of the time in church. However, being Greek Orthodox has never been simply a burdensome set of obligations to which the faithful must conform. Though there is a certain discipline that should be maintained through fasts and required ceremonies, Greek religious occasions are usually enjoyable, providing an excuse for merriment, dancing, and rejoicing. As described by Sanders, Greek religion "is supposed to be fun," and it accomplishes this through "the typically Greek device of finding a light touch in the midst of solemnity."[27] Indeed, most religious feasts involve music, dancing, and plenty of wine, much like the ancient feasts of sacrifice to the gods. During church ceremonies people tend to converse with one another, seemingly ignoring much of the ritual itself. Since there are no pews or benches in the church, and only a few stalls (without seats) along the wall for older attendees, there is a great deal of moving about during the ceremony. Worshipers come and go at will, participating when they feel the urge but not feeling an obligation to sit through what they find boring. This creates an atmosphere of informality not usually found in other highly ritualized churches. While outsiders might consider Greek church behavior irreverent, the Greek might argue that God is just as pleased by joy and frivolity as by more pious emotions and behaviors.

In Greece the metaphysical realm of the church is not confined to the community church but is extended into the home through the *iconostasi*, which is a shelf on which icons and other sacred objects are kept. Suspended in front of the icons is the *kandili*, or oil lamp, that may be lit by devout women every evening or perhaps only a few times during the year at major religious celebrations. The iconostasi is usually located in an eastern corner of the bedroom. As explained by Hirschon, this is a sacred space of concentrated spiritual presence, and through this presence the house itself becomes a temple, with the mother taking on the role of the priest by acting as the intercessor for the family and caring for its spiritual needs.[28]

Although Greek religion has its mystical aspects, it is deeply concerned with a person's daily life. Not only is it the mechanism though which individual action is directed to human need and affliction, but it is involved in all the important events of a person's life, from birth to baptism, from marriage to death. Particularly in times of death, religion helps reinforce the bonds that bind families to the rest of the community. Religious practices help people deal with the separation that death brings in a way that reinforces the social ties among the living.[29]

Perhaps it was only fitting that when the Roman Empire was divided into its Eastern and Western halves in A.D. 395, Greece, its philosophy and religion having so profoundly influenced the early church, would become heir to a new religion.[30] The Eastern half of the church adopted Greek as its official language, and most church officials were Greek. Though it sought at times to eliminate all vestiges of pagan influence from the culture, the church also played an important part in preserving ancient Greek culture and philosophy. Some say that the Renaissance in Europe started when Byzantine thinkers left the Greek world after its fall to the Ottomans and took the works of ancient Greeks with them to Europe. After Ottoman rule ended, ancient Greek philosophy returned to Greece through the Europeans who helped set up its first government and educational system. During the Ottoman period, Greek music, art, literature, and oral history were conserved by the churches and monasteries. In the years when the Ottomans ruled the country, it was the church that provided Greeks with a sense of unity and ethnic identity.

Elasticity and Tradition

Although their world is rapidly changing, interpersonal relations in Greece are contextually embedded in a traditional culture that will not disappear overnight. Outwardly, the village, the family, and the religion of Greeks may soon cease to resemble the past. Few young people remain in the villages to carry on the traditions. The cohesion of the family is threatened by pressures that arise when both spouses work outside the home. The church is competing with a trend toward secularism. However, the long and complex history of Greece has resulted in ways of thinking, social patterns, and communication styles that exhibit both strength and elasticity. The strength derives from a continuity with the past that exists despite many hardships and impositions from outside forces. The elasticity stems both from the constant need to adapt to changes and from the unique way in which the Greeks have resisted invaders.

In spite of the many times that outsiders have assumed control over the Greek people, the Greeks have never allowed themselves to be completely conquered. The Frankish crusaders and the Venetians left the stone walls of their fortresses throughout southern Greece, but little else remains from their long stay (other than a number of Greek Catholics on islands such as Tinos). Four hundred years of Ottoman rule gave the Greeks new clothing styles and put new foods on the table, but Greeks managed to maintain their language, religion, and connection to their ancient past. In most cases the conquerors of Greece left, having been changed by the Greeks to a much larger extent than they managed to exert influence over them. Under the Romans, Greek became the language of international trade and diplomacy, and Greek gods and goddesses were adopted under different names. The Christian church was influenced heavily by Greek philosophy, and as discussed earlier, the saints of the Orthodox Church may be the older Greek gods in disguise.

Today the invader is Western culture, and externally many Greeks follow a more contemporary Western lifestyle. It remains to be seen how the invasion of MTV, CNN, World Wide Web, and Western consumerism will influence Greek values, but the traveler who explores the Greek mosaic in the twenty-second century may find that the most recent onslaught will have left little more than a few scattered stones on the social landscape.

---

[1] According to Theophanis Manias, in his book *Unknown Great Achievements of the Ancient World* (Greek edition published in Athens, 1972, publisher unknown), in ancient Greece the letters of the alphabet were also used as numbers, so each letter had a corresponding numeric value. It was possible to sum the letters of a word to find a total. The distance from Sounion to the Parthenon was referred to as *asma*, which is the ancient word for "song." The sum of these letters is 242, which is the distance in stadia (1 stadia = 185 meters) between the temples. There are twenty-three other sites in the Attica and Biotia regions of Greece (in which Athens

is located) that were called asma and that have the same distance of 242 stadia between them. See also Wojciech W. Gasparski and Ioannes B. Kapelouzos, "A System behind the Ancient Greek Design" (paper presented at the conference on Cybernetics and Systems Research, held in Vienna in 1991).

[2] Michael Herzfeld, *Anthropology through the Looking-Glass* (Cambridge: Cambridge University Press, 1987), 2.

[3] William Davenport, *Athens* (New York: Time-Life Books), 1978.

[4] Pettifer, *The Greeks*, 149.

[5] Renee B. Hirschon, "Open Body/Closed Space: The Transformation of Female Sexuality," in *Defining Females*, edited by Shirley Ardener (New York: John Wiley and Sons, 1978), 73.

[6] Jill Dubisch, *Gender and Power in Rural Greece* (Princeton, NJ: Princeton University Press, 1986).

[7] Hirschon, "Open Body/Closed Space," 74.

[8] Harry C. Triandis, *The Analysis of Subjective Culture* (New York: John Wiley and Sons, 1972), 310.

[9] Hirschon, "Open Body/Closed Space," 75.

[10] Triandis, *Subjective Culture*, 306.

[11] This taking of children is viewed very differently by those with opposing political affiliations. My friends on the left insist that the retreating andartes took only their own children and perhaps those of friends and family who volunteered. Others refer to it as another pedomazoma, in which most of the children were taken unwillingly.

[12] Irvin T. Sanders, *Rainbow in the Rock: The People of Rural Greece* (Cambridge: Harvard University Press, 1962), 129.

[13] Hirschon, "Open Body/Closed Space," 75.

[14] *Poniros* is generally not considered a "good" word, and it should not be used by the foreigner to refer to anyone.

[15] Dorothy Lee, *Freedom and Culture* (Englewood Cliffs, NJ: Prentice-Hall, 1959), 149.

[16] *Area Handbook for Greece* (Washington, DC: American University, 1970), 78-79.

[17] Nicholas Gage, *Hellas: A Portrait of Greece* (Athens: Efstathiadis Group, 1987), 33-34.

[18] Younger women of marriageable age in Greece are beginning to change significantly their expectations for marriage. Several

young women I spoke with emphasized that their future husband would support them in their professional interests and would share the household chores and upbringing of children. However, when I asked one of my friends if it would be possible for a young Greek woman to find a young Greek man who shared this view, he quickly replied, "If she does, he won't be Greek." He was implying both that it would be difficult to find a young man of this type and that if such a person existed, he has lost his Greek culture.

[19] Hart, *Time, Religion, and Social Experience in Rural Greece.*

[20] Sanders, *Rainbow in the Rock,* 265.

[21] *Greece: A Country Study* (Washington, DC: American University, 1985), ch. 4.

[22] Fermor, *Mani,* 214.

[23] Sanders, *Rainbow in the Rock,* 260.

[24] The tiny shrines along roadsides may also be placed there because there has been an accident at that location. Sometimes the shrine is a sign of thankfulness for sparing the life of the accident victim, and at other times it is a memorial to the one who was killed.

[25] Sanders, *Rainbow in the Rock,* 259.

[26] Fermor, *Mani,* 219.

[27] Sanders, *Rainbow in the Rock,* 258.

[28] Renee B. Hirschon, "Essential Objects and the Sacred: Interior and Exterior Space in an Urban Locality," in *Women and Space,* edited by Shirley Ardener (London: Droom Helm, 1981), 80.

[29] Sanders, *Rainbow in the Rock,* 272.

[30] See A. H. Armstrong and R. A. Markus, *Christian Faith and Greek Philosophy* (London: Darton, Longman and Todd, 1960).

4

The Greek Way

On a recent spring day that brought a deep blue sky and warm sunshine over Athens, I enjoyed a walk on the slopes of Mt. Imitos, one of the three mountains surrounding the city. There I followed a small trail that wound its way up the mountainside through a pine forest and then across the steep, open, rocky terrain. Along the way were marvelous views of Athens and the surrounding valley, including the Saronic Gulf and nearby islands as well as the mountains of the Peloponnese in the far distance. In full view was the Acropolis and the magnificent Parthenon that crowns this famous promontory.

As I climbed to the top of Mt. Imitos, I considered just how much this trail reminded me of the Greek way of life. First, the trail was not included on any map or as part of any listing of trails that I had previously encountered. In a similar manner, so much of what I have learned about the way of life in Greece came by accident and not from an organized source. Discovery by exploration is perhaps the only way to truly come into contact with Greek values and perspectives. Second, the trail traversed drastically different types of terrain, at times easing its way along a gentle path beneath a shaded forest of pine trees and at other times bumping over rough rock outcroppings exposed to the strong afternoon sun. Relations between Greeks are similar in their stark contrasts, characterized by alternating periods of peaceful cooperation and intense strife. The traveler navigating the Greek interpersonal landscape must be prepared for sudden and often extreme changes in emotional footing. Third, the trail offered dramatic views in almost all directions, providing a striking perspective on the city of Athens and its surrounding area. By analogy, the difficulty of navigating the social world of the Greeks is rewarded by new and exciting perspectives on human values and activities.

Contradictions and Paradoxes

To make statements about the Greek way of life is a daunting and dangerous challenge. Almost everything that can be said about the nature of Greeks and Greek society can be paired with an opposite statement that is equally true. In order to gain insight into the Greek way of thinking, one must be willing to accept apparent contradictions and paradoxes. The Greeks are almost impossible to classify, as the following passage from a Greek newspaper so vividly states:

> The Greek is most intelligent but he is also arrogant; he is active but he lacks method; he is "philotimos" [see later discussion in this chapter] but he is also full of prejudices; he is hot-blooded but he is a fighter as well. He built the Parthenon and getting drunk from its glory he allowed it later to become a target of quarrels; he gave rise to Socrates in order to poison him; he exalted Themistocles in order to expel him; he followed [the teachings of] Aristotle in order to push him away; he gave birth to Venizelos in order to assassinate him. He built Byzantium in order to give it to the Turks; he brought about 1821 [war for independence from the Ottoman Empire] in order to endanger it; he created 1909 [a military coup] in order to forget it. He tripled the size of Greece and he almost buried it; one moment he is fighting for truth and another moment he hates those who refuse to serve

lies. The Greek: a paradoxical creature, untamed, curious, semi-good, semi-bad, one of uncertain dispositions, selfish and wise-foolish. Pity him or admire him, if you want. Classify him...if you can![1]

Because the Greek way of life in general is difficult to capture, any attempt to provide a description of the Greek way of thinking will be less than complete. Nevertheless, it is important to consider some fundamental concepts that form the basis for Greek social relations.[2] Exposure to these concepts may help the visitor to Greece better comprehend the confusing sights and sounds that are likely to be encountered.

Greeks and Barbarians

When I speak of the friends that I have developed in Greece, I often use the word *family* to describe my relationship to them, particularly those with whom I have maintained close contact over the years. Indeed, the ties that bind us are as strong as those that link most families, and the mutual obligations that exist between us require actions that rarely exist between close friends in the United States. For example, during the past ten years, I have not stayed in a hotel even once while visiting Athens. Each time I made the trip to Greece, several of my friends would insist that I stay in their homes. Because there is barely enough space in their houses for their own families, they often moved out of their bedrooms to give me a place to sleep. I found that I could not protest by telling them I didn't want to cause them so much trouble, because in their mind my stay was not viewed in this manner at all. They expected that I would stay with them, and my refusal would be a true insult. This responsibility to my well-being extends far beyond staying in their homes. I am provided a great deal of protection and support, with continuous offers of assistance and constant companionship.

Although my own experiences have been overwhelmingly positive, I seldom find that other foreigners who have lived, worked, or traveled in Greece remember their stay so fondly. While some tend to find the people of their host country refreshingly warm and hospitable, as I have, a large percentage recall the Greeks as uncomfortably rude and uncaring. How can similar circumstances result in such contrasting experiences? Perhaps this discrepancy can be understood best by exploring how Greeks behave differently toward members of the *ingroup* and the *outgroup*. Like other aspects of Greek society, this differentiation can be traced to ancient times, as a look at Homer's *Odyssey* reveals.

Odysseus was portrayed as a just, fair, and kind man, ruling his people in an exemplary manner. Indeed, he was true to his friends at all costs, loyal to his followers, hospitable and courteous to his guests, and he treated all his workers in a humane and compassionate manner. Yet, he was praised for his sacking of the city of Ismarus on the Thracian coast, where he killed the men and divided their wives and wealth among himself and his followers. This raid on a city which had done nothing to offend Odysseus or any of his followers was considered permissible because the inhabitants were not Greek and therefore did not fall within the boundaries of Greek justice. Even in the golden age of Greek democracy (446-31 B.C.), Athenians divided their world into Greeks and barbarians, a barbarian being anyone who did not share Greek culture and language.

While the concept of justice among Greeks today is certainly much different from that in Homer's world, the distinction between ingroup and outgroup is still strong and affects significantly how Greeks relate to others. In the view of Triandis, Greeks define their universe in terms of the triumphs of the ingroup over the outgroup.[3] As is true for most societies, the distinction between these two groups affects relations with people in a wide variety of situations, including interaction with foreign visitors. Although this distinction is not unique to Greek society, the strength of commitment to ingroup members and the degree of indifference, and sometimes even hostility, exhibited toward outgroup members is much stronger than is usually found in Western countries.[4]

For Greeks, the ingroup includes family, relatives, friends, and even friends of friends. Guests and other people who are perceived as warm, caring, and willing to help quickly become friends and thus part of the ingroup. Outgroup members include those in the community outside the immediate and the extended family and the network of ingroup affiliations as well as guests who fail to demonstrate sensitivity and consideration for the concerns of their hosts. A great deal of commitment exists between ingroup members, requiring intimacy, concern, and good conduct. Feelings of trust, support, cooperation, sympathy, and admiration are exchanged frequently among members of the ingroup. In the context of a highly competitive social world, the ingroup provides protection and help for its members.

Relations with outgroup members, on the other hand, are characterized by suspicion and mistrust. Very little commitment is felt toward entities not part of the ingroup, and influence and pressure from the outgroup are rejected. This affects numerous areas of Greek social and political life, ranging from relations with neighbors to responsibility felt toward the state. In the United States it is common for housing communities to organize cleanup days or neighborhood watch programs to deter crime. Community programs of this type are rarely found in Greece, since such participation is dependent on a sense of responsibility to a generalized community of strangers who are not part of the ingroup. Even the relationship between authority figures and subordinates is dependent on ingroup/outgroup considerations. For example, in larger organizations managers are often viewed by employees as part of the outgroup, and in this case they are avoided and treated with hostility. If, on the other hand, managers come to be identified as part of the ingroup, they are responded to with submissiveness, acceptance, and warmth.

The suspicion and mistrust of outgroup members lead to a general lack of helpfulness toward them. This is illustrated in a study by Triandis, who compared how people in the United States, Europe, and Greece behave toward foreign strangers and how they behave toward strangers who are fellow nationals. In one situation, where the stranger asked for help from a local, approximately 50 percent of those asked in Europe and the United States provided the assistance, regardless of whether the request came from a foreigner or a fellow national. In Greece, however, this degree of help was only provided to the foreigner (a potential ingroup member) requesting assistance. Only 10 percent of locals agreed to help a fellow Greek whom they did not know, as this person was clearly an outgroup member.[5]

Concealment and deception often come into play in relations with the outgroup. These can serve as a means for upholding ingroup and family honor and prestige. In a world where honor must be protected and competition is a way of life, deception is sometimes a useful means of fulfilling one's duties. The phrase "You can't live without lies" is reported by sociologists as often heard in villages, where the word for "lies," *psemata*, is used with less emotional intensity and does not have the overtones of morality found in English. Psemata are strongly condemned on the conscious level, however, and children are urged to avoid being untruthful in their dealings with others. Nevertheless, the use of psemata is often justified as necessary under certain circumstances. For example, there is very little sense of personal responsibility for the welfare of the state, resulting in a major problem for government officials in the collection of income taxes. For most people, it is more important to hide income from the government, so that it can be used for the family, than it is to contribute to a strong national economy.

Cheating, while it is completely unacceptable within the

ingroup, is acceptable when it is directed toward members of the outgroup. In such cases, cheating is treated in the context of competition, where it is acceptable that the outgroup member be taken advantage of if he or she is weak—so one is expected to be on guard against cheating. During my first teaching experience in Greece, students immediately tested me by all sorts of both clever and clumsy attempts to cheat. Those who knew the material well helped others who were not prepared, and many students pulled out notes hidden between papers, under skirts, taped beneath desks, and so on. None of my arguments about the detrimental effects of cheating on the learning process had an impact on the students' behavior. Particularly ineffective were arguments that the good students were only hurting themselves by sharing information with their friends. Of course, what I did not understand at the time was that the good students felt an obligation to help their friends, and the entire class felt it only natural to try and deceive the teacher. I gained an initial reprieve when I tricked the students with an exam in which all copies appeared the same but were in fact different, causing those who copied their friends' answers to earn extremely low scores. This helped establish the new teacher as a more formidable force, against whom cheating might not be worth the effort. However, it was only after I established rapport with many of the students and came to be viewed as a part of the ingroup that the cheating ceased.

Fortunately, mechanisms exist that provide sanctions for negative behaviors when they go beyond reasonable limits. There exists a code of behavior that condemns lying, cheating, gossiping, and so on, and while engaging in these behaviors, one must not do anything to bring shame to the ingroup. Because the honor of the family must be upheld, it is important not to go too far with one's deviousness. Since most families strive to develop and uphold a good reputation, none want to be known as the seat of lies or the source of corruption. Therefore, within the ingroup itself, there is usually pressure to keep distortion, deception, and other actions against the outgroup under control. Thus, the chronic gossip is disapproved of, the habitual liar is no longer believed, and those who constantly cheat are made to feel ashamed.[6]

The strength and the nature of the ingroup/outgroup distinction in Greece form the background against which many of the dramas of daily life are acted out. Loyalty to the former and feelings ranging from mild disregard to intense animosity for the latter provide the background upon which many conflicts are staged. In order to adequately understand the tension that characterizes interpersonal relationships in Greece, however, it is necessary to explore the Greek sense of self, especially as it is tied to ingroup behavior.

Philotimo: *The Essence of Greek Character*

Perhaps the most cherished term for a Greek is *eleftheria*, which means "freedom." Yet for much of its long and sometimes glorious history Greece has been subjected to foreign domination—for four hundred years under the Ottoman Empire and most recently, during the Second World War, under Nazi Germany. Despite this history of domination by external forces, Greeks have maintained a strong sense of personal freedom, transcending circumstances. While there are many factors that contribute to the Greeks' ability to keep a vision of freedom before them under very difficult conditions, the most important influence is every person's strong sense of *philotimo*, a central aspect of self-definition.

Although it translates literally as "love of honor," philotimo is not captured adequately with any English word or phrase; it is a concept that refers to several aspects of Greek character and social relations. First is a sense of responsibility and obligation to the ingroup, particularly to the family, the most important social unit in Greece. Greeks are obliged to uphold the family honor and to provide assistance to family members. This extends in various ways to other members of the ingroup. It is one's duty to take care of family and friends first when one has resources such as employment or material goods to distribute. Thus, Greeks find it difficult to be impartial when they are in positions of authority. They feel obliged to offer jobs to cousins, sons of friends, and other ingroup members, irrespective of their skills or qualifications or how they might be ranked in comparison with other applicants. In turn, those who are given this preferential treatment feel a strong sense of loyalty to their employer and are likely to be more dedicated to the mission of the company.

Second, philotimo refers to appropriate behavior within the ingroup. As Triandis indicates, a person who is considered philotimos behaves toward members of his ingroup in a way that is "polite, virtuous, reliable, proud,...truthful, generous, self-sacrificing, tactful, respectful, and grateful."[7] Philotimo requires a person to sacrifice him- or herself to help family or friends and to avoid doing or saying things that reflect negatively on them. Appropriate behavior should be seen and felt, not only by the ingroup but by the outgroup as well, thus increasing prestige for the former in the eyes of the latter.

Third, philotimo is strongly related to a person's sense of personal honor and self-esteem. As anthropologist Dorothy Lee has described it, "Foremost in the Greek's view of the self is his self-esteem. It is impossible to have good relations with Greeks unless one is aware of this, the Greek *philotimo*. It is important to pay tribute to it and to avoid offending it, or as the Greeks say, molesting it."[8] The Greek philotimo is easily bruised, and there is constant emphasis on both protecting and enhancing philotimo. Protecting it leads to a concern with losing face, with shielding the inner core of the self from ridicule, and with avoiding actions that would cause loss of respect. One is always on guard against being outsmarted by the outgroup, and it is seldom that Greeks put themselves in a position where they are in less than full control of their senses in order to avoid personal abuse and damage to the ingroup. Thus, even though alcohol is a part of almost every meal and social event, one rarely sees Greeks become drunk, and until now drugs have not become a major problem in the country.

Offense against one's philotimo brings retaliation against the offender rather than feelings of self-criticism or self-blame. The avoidance of self-blame does not have the connotation of irresponsibility because it is a necessary part of the maintenance of self-esteem. In the same vein, philotimo is not related to feelings of remorse or guilt, and it is not strongly tied to notions of ethical morality. If actions are taken in defense of philotimo that bring harm to outgroup members, responsibility is not accepted for what occurs following the actions. If the demands of philotimo have been satisfied, the person taking action against others is entitled to reject any blame for subsequent misfortune.

The safeguarding of philotimo promotes a sense of equality between individuals, and thus it is seldom that one Greek feels inferior to another. Even differences in status level and role responsibility are not cast in terms of superiority or inferiority in Greece. Every public servant, farmer, or waiter feels comfortable telling his or her boss, or even the prime minister, how to run things. However, the philotimo of the Greek is different from an individual sense of pride. It is promoted by actions that bring honor and respect to the family and the ingroup, whereas the expression of pride connotes arrogance, which is detested by the Greeks. A common proverb states that "the clever (proud) bird is caught by the nose."

Philotimo is the key to behavior within the ingroup, and it frames much of one's behavior toward the outgroup. Requirements of philotimo lead to actions that enhance the position of the ingroup and, at the same time, trigger actions in its defense. Because of the demands of philotimo, interpersonal relationships tend to be characterized by competitiveness, struggle, and conflict. These conflicts can continue over long periods of time and at a high level of intensity without feelings of guilt or remorse. While such conflicts are usually viewed in negative terms by Westerners, they play an important and often positive role in Greek social relations. In many ways, the energy that conflicts generate provides the stimulus for dealing with the demands of the ingroup and for confronting the challenges of the outgroup.

Interpersonal Tension and Struggle

When I first lived in Athens in the early 1980s, our apartment shared a wall with a couple in their thirties with two small children. To our unaccustomed ears, it seemed that the couple was constantly engaged in intense argument, either between the two of them or with their children. The same was true when neighbors visited them; the level and tone of their voices carried through the wall in a loud, combative, and sometimes hostile manner. In our naiveté we felt bad for the couple and for the children, caught up (we presumed) in a contentious family. As we slowly discovered, the sounds we heard from our neighbors were not arguments but rather normal conversation on everyday topics. The couple had a healthy relationship and the children were well adjusted. Our mistake was one we were to see foreigners make over and over as they first entered the Greek interpersonal landscape.

Permeating almost every facet of daily life in Greece is a sense of contest. Very little goes unchallenged, and everyone takes seriously the maxim that the unexamined utterance is not worth hearing. However, for Greeks, this struggle brings with it feelings of stimulation, excitement, and genuine human contact. The painful feelings that are often the result of conflict are not viewed as aberrations but as part of the natural course of human relations. In Greece, conflict is an aspect of everyday transactions that is unavoidable.

Ernestine Friedl, in describing life in a traditional Greek village in the 1960s, reports that when one walks through the fields and inquires about how the work is going, the people

generally respond with *"Palevoume"* ("We are struggling").[9]
The villagers' use of the verb *palevo* expresses the difficult
conditions confronting farmers trying to make a living from
the predominately rocky soil and mountainous terrain. At
the same time, it reflects the predominant worldview and
orientation toward interpersonal relations that are characteristic of Greek reality. Sociologists report that even a positive
term like *success* is linked by Greeks with struggle, whereas
for those in the United States it is linked with careful planning and hard work. Greece has been described as a place
with "joy and tragedy straight out of Aeschylus, Sophocles,
and Euripides, and it is expressed with...the same tendency
to use strong words and violent gestures;...the same warm
heart, the disdain for time, and the delight in life lived fully,
with all the senses awake."[10]

While Greece is a land of unparalleled scenic beauty, it is
also a land of contrasts. Physically, the mountains and the sea
meet each other throughout the country, often resulting in
dramatic settings. Culturally, there are contrasts between the
island inhabitants and the mountain villagers. Historically,
the Greek character has always fought over the opposing
poles of a feminine Ionian nature and a masculine Dorian
persona. Geographically, Greece sits between the Near East
and Europe and has been invaded and occupied by forces
from both, resulting in cultural influences from East and
West. Politically, there have been swings between military
dictatorships and socialist governments, although the dictatorships did not come about by choice of the people. These
contrasts and the resulting struggle between opposites is
deeply embedded in the nature of Greek reality.

> Greek identity as a whole [is] best seen as a constant oscilla-
> tion between just such opposites as these. The spirit and the
> flesh, ideal and reality, triumph and despair—you name them
> and the Greeks suffer or enjoy them as the constant poles of
> their being, swinging repeatedly from one to the other and
> back again, often contriving to embrace both poles simulta-

neously, but above all never reconciled, never contented, never still. *This perennial sense of tension between diametrically opposed forces is the essence of their existence*—the one absolutely consistent feature of their identity since Greek history began. In the phrase of the Cretan novelist, Kazantzakis, they are truly double-born souls.[11]

This tension is expressed in many ways, especially in communication style and competition within relationships.

Communication Style and the Role of Kouvenda

The communication style of Greeks has been described as "contrapuntal virtuosity, incisive, combative, loud."[12] To the unaccustomed ear, every conversation appears to be an argument, and gentleness seems to play no part in dialogue. The substance of conversation is less important than the style, because it is the process that counts. Discussion has been described as "a battle of personal opinion, and its end is neither to reach the truth nor to reach a conclusion; its end is sheer enjoyment of vigorous speech."[13] Indeed, the Western visitor to Greece is immediately struck by the intensity of the verbal exchanges.

> A city neighborhood or a village can be compared to a stage, and friends, neighbors, and kin to a Greek chorus commenting on unfolding marriages, hospitality, or sexual infidelity. No one can remain solely in the audience, however; neutrality is impossible to maintain. No one can expect to receive support of his or her reputation unless he or she defends that of allies. Manipulation of opinion depends on gossip, which in turn depends on the breaking of confidences, amusement derived from ridicule, and malicious attempts to exploit the situation.[14]

Challenges, insults, and attacks are, within appropriate limits, almost synonymous with conversing. Writers say that conversation "has some of the quality of an arena in which each man displays himself as an individual and waits for an audience response. People talk at each other rather than with each other"[15] It is not unusual for several monologues to be going on simultaneously at a table as different individuals struggle to hold center stage and assert their personalities.

Kouvenda, or conversation, is extremely important in Greek society. As Triandis says, "Greeks love to discuss, to argue, and to match their wits with other debaters."[16] To "exercise the tongue and provoke the mind" is seen by some as "the most fulfilling pastime of all."[17] Athens is a city where social activity—eating out, drinking, dancing, singing, and, above all, conversing—permeates everyday life to an extraordinary degree. From childhood, everyone receives a great deal of verbal stimulation, for the ability to hold one's own in discussion is a skill that no one can live without.

Kouvenda has a number of important functions in Greek society. First, it is through conversation that personal relationships are developed and maintained. Establishing a social bond through conversation allows individuals to place each other within the ingroup, thus promoting warmer feelings and a greater degree of trust. Hirschon says that "company with others has an intrinsic value, solitude is abhorred and the personality type most approved is that of the open and warm individual, while someone described as closed is also seen as cold."[18] Isolation and withdrawal, she says, are equivalent to social death; to engage in verbal exchange is thus a recognition of the other's existence.

Second, kouvenda is a means of asserting a sense of equality in encounters with others. This equality is not necessarily related to equality of status, education, or economic level, but rather it refers to equality as a human being. As Friedl emphasizes, "The right to a certain give-and-take underlies all relationships and serves to keep each situation unique and each relationship one of equality on at least some level."[19] This equality is demanded by one's philotimo, and it is through kouvenda that it is established and maintained. It may lead one to present strong views on a topic with which one is unfamiliar and then to defend these views stubbornly even in the face of clear evidence to the contrary. To lose an argument on the basis of facts or logic presented by the other person would show weakness and would put one in an inferior position. Asserting one's personality by providing strong opinions and engaging in sometimes heated argument is a common means of elevating the philotimo on an individual level.

Third, kouvenda provides a source of entertainment. Traditional village life is routine and repetitive, and especially before the advent of television, it was through conversation that freshness and uniqueness were brought to commonplace events. Variation and uncertainty are imposed on aspects of life that otherwise have no intrinsically adventurous elements. Entertainment is enhanced by the rich oral tradition of the Greeks, whose language allows a precision of expression that promotes unsurpassed storytelling. Today, everyday language is still rich in proverbs, myths, legends, and humor, even among the uneducated. Holden shows how boasting sometimes takes the form of "apparently harmless rhetorical embroidery to make actual situations seem grander, more significant and more self-flattering than they really are."[20]

Finally, kouvenda is important in asserting one's personality and maintaining self-esteem. Social life is vital because prestige and reputation, which depend on the opinion of others, are the measure of both the individual's merit and that of his or her family. Kouvenda is the way men and women boast of their own and their family's achievements and is the vehicle for men to display their political knowledge and engage in political argument. Boasting is socially acceptable and may be a means of promoting philotimo.

Despite the high level of intensity reflected in kouvenda, arguments, debates, and other verbal disputes are not viewed as aberrations, and they do not necessarily affect relationships negatively or lead to negative feelings within relationships. Rather, they are viewed as integral aspects of daily existence. Kouvenda, while it reflects the interpersonal struggle that is the essence of Greek reality, functions on center stage, in full view of any audience. Behind the scenes lies relational struggle, in which rivalry and competition play key roles.

Competition and Relational Struggle

Many writers have discussed the deep current of rivalry and suspicion among Greeks. Relationships are in a constant state of flux because of the competitive nature of the Greeks' social orientation. As one popular phrase expresses it, *Kalitera na se misoun para na se lipounde*, or "It is better to be hated than to be pitied." Greeks tend to believe that "the friend of my enemy is my enemy, and the enemy of my enemy is my friend," so they are constantly making, dissolving, and remaking coalitions as different "enemies" appear on the scene.

The ongoing struggles in Greek social life are fueled by a competitive orientation different from that found in most Western societies. It is often noted that whereas in Europe and the United States people compete with each other by trying to "run faster" to get ahead of the other, the Greeks compete with each other by grabbing onto their competitors to hold them back, thus keeping them from getting ahead. While the following story, provided by Costas Sophoulis, professor at the University of the Aegean, somewhat over-states the situation for the sake of illustration, it depicts the primary difference between the Greek approach to competition and the approach more typical of the West.

God chose four good men and decided to give each of them a wish, because they had lived such good lives. One man was from Germany, one from France, one from England and one from Greece. When God asked the German for his favor, the German requested a good gun. When God asked why, the German replied that he wanted a good gun because his neighbor had a nice one, and he did not want to be left with less than his neighbor. The French asked for a good bottle of wine, because his neighbor drank such fine wines and he felt left out. The Englishman asked for a new overcoat, again to keep up with his neighbor. Finally, God asked the Greek for his wish, and he asked God to kill his neighbor's donkey. Puzzled, God asked why, and the Greek replied: "Because I have no donkey and it is not good for my neighbor to have something I don't."

The tendency to compete by bringing down one's foe signals a different approach to conflict that can significantly affect the manner in which interpersonal struggles are managed. Moreover, the requirements of philotimo and the distinction between ingroup and outgroup create a situation in which relationships within the community are polarized. According to Mariella Doumanis, in traditional Greek communities "social relationships were either positive or negative, with no room for neutral gradation in between. Families were either cooperating with one another, closely and intimately, or were competing aggressively, cunningly and sometimes fiercely."[21]

Tension and the Sense of Being Alive

The interpersonal struggle characteristic of Greek relationships is not totally focused on *outcome* but rather tends to center on *process*. Heard often is the phrase *perasmena, ksehasmena*, or "What is past is forgotten." Applying not only to unpleasant events but equally to success, it points to the short-lived nature of both victory and defeat. The need for constant stimulation is strong, so the prospect of life without a competitor generally seems intolerable. Thus, new relational struggles are constantly developing.

It can be argued that interpersonal battles provide a great deal of personal and social satisfaction to Greeks. Perhaps it is the continuing *agonia* (anxiety or agony) that provides for the Greek a feeling of being alive. Holden describes conflict as "generating the leaping spark of tension that is the only certain characteristic of Greekness. Tension, movement, change, process; these are the essence of Greek life."[22] Indeed, somewhat like the many species of fish that would simply die if the water currents did not constantly flow through their gills, constant change may be the essence of Greek identity.

Not only do struggles provide some degree of stimulation and satisfaction for Greeks, they also play an important role in strengthening ingroup solidarity. The hostility and opposition directed toward the outgroup serves as a complement to the cooperation necessary within the ingroup. Through competition with the outgroup, ingroup members attest to their allegiance to the ingroup. As pointed out by Doumanis, "The values of prestige and honor so central in the traditional Greek culture rested on the attention and opinion of friends *and* enemies, on the concerned interest of kin *and* the grudging acceptance of competitors."[23]

Personal relationships and interpersonal communication in Greece mirror the contrasts found in the physical landscape. Just as the Greek countryside is dominated by mountainous and often rough terrain, conversations and relationships are characterized by transactions that seem to the outsider harsh and rocky. Physical, spiritual, and social struggles are built into the Greek landscape, psyche, and relationships in ways that are difficult for the Western mind to comprehend. Although these struggles would exhaust the Westerner, they invigorate the Greek. Only by understanding the role and function of interpersonal struggle and conflict can the outsider begin to comprehend the competition and rivalry that characterize the turbulent world of relationships in Greece.

---

[1] This is a translation of an excerpt from a Greek newspaper, originally provided to me by a Greek friend. I recently learned that

the original piece was written by an American judge, N. Kelly, and won a prize in a competition sponsored by an unnamed magazine in Chicago in 1938.

[2] Portions of the discussion in this chapter are taken from the author's previously published article, "Palevoume: Struggle and Conflict in Greek Interpersonal Relations," *Southern Communication Journal* 55 (Spring 1990): 260-75.

[3] Triandis, *Subjective Culture*, 299.

[4] It is important to note that the strong ingroup/outgroup distinctions in Greece do not imply that Greeks are more collectivist in their social orientation. Rather, Greeks are highly individualistic in their behavior, yet at the same time they are deeply committed to the well-being of fellow ingroup members.

[5] In Greece a foreign stranger is a potential ingroup member because of the emphasis the culture places on *philoxenia*, or kindness to strangers.

[6] Juliet du Boulay, "Lies, Mockery and Family Integrity," in *Mediterranean Family Structure*, edited by J. G. Peristiany (New York: Cambridge University Press, 1976), 399-400.

[7] Triandis, *Subjective Culture*, 308-09.

[8] Lee, *Freedom and Culture*, 141.

[9] Ernestine Friedl, *Vasilika: A Village in Modern Greece* (New York: Holt, Rinehart and Winston, 1962).

[10] Gage, *Hellas*, 24.

[11] Holden, *Greece without Columns*, 27-28 (emphasis mine).

[12] Lee, *Freedom and Culture*, 146.

[13] Ibid., 146.

[14] *Greece: A Country Study*, 145.

[15] Friedl, *Vasilika*, 83.

[16] Triandis, *Subjective Culture*, 323.

[17] Gage, *Hellas*, 30.

[18] Hirschon, "Open Body/Closed Space," 77.

[19] Friedl, *Vasilika*, 83.

[20] Holden, *Greece without Columns*, 94.

[21] Mariella Doumanis, *Mothering in Greece: From Collectivism to Individualism* (London: Academic Press, 1983), 28.

[22] Holden, *Greece without Columns*, 33.

[23] Doumanis, *Mothering in Greece*, 29 (emphasis mine).

5

The Rhythm of Work

In an interview with the top manager of the development arm of Greece's commercial bank, I was told that the primary difference between Greek and foreign management styles is that "in Greece you must manage persons, not personnel." Over the next two hours I was to see just what he meant by this statement. His door was never closed while I was in his office, and people were constantly coming and going. Some of the visitors were division chiefs who wanted his advice or approval before moving forward with some action for which they had been assigned responsibility. Some were secretaries or other support persons who wanted to ask a favor, or for time away from the office for shopping, or to let him know about someone's upcoming birthday or family event. One caller was his driver, there to give his advice about an important investment decision the bank was about to make. A couple of times the manager left the office briefly to talk with colleagues he saw passing in the hall. He had a special phone on his desk that his family used to call him, which they did twice while I was present.

As I interviewed other Greek managers, I often encountered a similar pattern of behavior. It became apparent that it would be difficult for managers and other professionals from the United States to work in this way. We would have trouble with the constant interruptions, the hesitancy of subordinates to act on their own initiative when they have been delegated responsibility, the need to deal with so many personal situations of subordinates, and the frequent calls from family while at work. Our task-centered approach to work, our need to use time "productively," our friendly but distant relations with employees and colleagues, our emphasis on efficiency, our need for structure, and our strict separation of family and work concerns would cause us endless frustrations. In order to be successful in dealing with Greek colleagues and subordinates, there are several aspects of the work environment that are important to understand.

Attitudes toward Work

For most people in the United States, particularly for managers and professionals, work is a meaningful source of identity. With our achievement orientation, we depend significantly on work to bring us personal satisfaction. Much of our status comes from the work we do, and we devote a considerable amount of thought in our younger years to figuring out what work we will do when we are older. Indeed, the very question "What do you want to be when you grow up?" equates one's being with one's work. We spend a great deal of time outside of work talking about our jobs, and "What do you do?" is one of the first questions asked of a new acquaintance. Given these attitudes toward work, it is not surprising that we are willing to sacrifice so much of our personal and family life for the sake of our job.

At one level, there are many similarities between the U.S. and the Greek approach to work. Greeks share an action or "doing" orientation that stresses the need to work hard and struggle in order to better one's life. Many of my friends work extremely long hours, some of them holding down two different jobs. There is a professional class that derives personal satisfaction from the work they do, although this group is probably not large. Greeks are also materialistic, although material possessions are important not so much for their utilitarian value as for their prestige.

On another level, however, there is a different approach to work than one finds in the United States. In the Greek language there are two words that can be used to refer to work. The word *ergasia* is positive, and people speak with pride when they use it to refer to what they do. It means one's occupation, profession, or trade, and it can be used to refer to a work of art. However, most people today refer to their work as *doulia*, a word which also means "slavery" and "bondage." It is difficult to speak with pride or enthusiasm when thinking how one slaves away at the job!

Although Greeks are hardworking people when the situation requires, they do not see hard work as an end in itself. As Lee wrote many years ago,

> it is the personal quality of diligence, not work itself, which is good. To work compulsively is to be a slave to work; and what can be worse than slavery? Even to work under the compulsion of work as a virtue is to deny oneself prized freedom; all work under pressure, such as the pressure of a time limit or the dictates of an employer, means loss of freedom. Industrialization and work in urban centers usually run counter to this value.[1]

For most Greeks, work is something you do that is important, but its place in the overall scheme of things is balanced against other aspects of life that have greater value. The nature of one's work has little to do with personal identity, although some professions certainly have higher status than others. As often happens in the United States, Greeks ask their children about the kind of work they will do when they are grown, but the emphasis tends to be placed on how much money they will make or how much status they will gain rather than on what they will "be." Outside the job, Greeks don't talk much about their work with friends or family, and knowing the nature of another's work is not an important question in the initial stages of a relationship. Although the type of work one performs eventually becomes an appropriate topic for conversation, on several occasions I have been a guest in the home of a new acquaintance and my job was never raised as a subject of conversation during the course of a long dinner and evening together.[2]

For Greeks, the family clearly takes precedence over work. Whereas in the United States we are likely to bring our work home, the Greek is more likely to bring home to work. Not many managers are like my friend in the development bank with a special telephone line in the office for family calls, but family concerns affect the work environment. For example, it is common for people to take time off to deal with personal matters. Moreover, Greeks will quickly tell you that it is for their family that they work so hard. Most people are willing to put up with undesirable jobs if it means increased security for the family. However, it is very unlikely that the individual will feel greater loyalty to the company or to his or her career than to the family. Rarely will a Greek uproot the family in order to take a better position elsewhere.

Individualism and Egalitarianism

Although the United States is known for its rugged individualism and love of personal freedom, it is the Greeks who first developed these characteristics to their highest level, and they have not yet been dethroned. Perhaps more than any other people on the planet, Greeks are extremely individualistic and fiercely independent.[3] The word for "person," *atomo*, comes from the word for "atom," which was believed by ancient Greek scientists to be the indivisible unit of the universe. As Fermor describes it, "Every Greek may be said to comprise a one-man splinter-group."[4]

This "hyper-individualism," as it was dubbed in a recent article in the *Economist*,[5] manifests itself in several ways in the work environment. First, Greeks do not like to be managed or controlled by a company. They prefer to work for themselves. *Afentiko*, the word for "boss," means "master," and while it is sometimes used by workers as an endearing term for their boss, it has connotations similar to the master-slave relationship. *Thelo na ime afentiko tou eaftou mou*, one hears the Greeks say, or "I want to be my own boss." About half of the labor force is self-employed, and 90 percent of Greek firms have fewer than ten workers.[6] There is a strong distaste for the impersonal nature of large corporate organizations, and cooperative ventures in agriculture have been slow to be accepted. Businesses are run on the conviction that it is more profitable and more secure to keep them within the family. There is also a strong sense of obligation to provide for and accommodate the interests of immediate family members and their relatives. There is a reluctance to expand an enterprise if doing so means seeking outside capital or putting outsiders in positions of trust and authority. It is unlikely that an individual will invest capital in enterprises in which there are no family connections.[7]

Second, Greeks are not the least bit intimidated by status or hierarchy. Every individual has a strong opinion about how things should be done and doesn't hesitate to let that opinion be known. The driver in this chapter's opening example who came into the manager's office to give his advice on an important bank investment was no exception. Many people have commented about the high opinion Greeks seem to hold of themselves and how they seem to believe that only their unique contribution can lead the company to prosperity. If given the opportunity, most Greeks will become heavily engaged in the affairs of the company for which they work. As one writer suggests,

> Greeks are, indeed, not only natural participators but compulsive egalitarians as well.... Rank, class or status mean little to them as a rule, except as indications of the personal advan-

tage that may be gained from striking up an acquaintance with a person of title or connection.... Normally they expect everyone from the Prime Minister downwards to maintain an open door to them at all times....[8]

Of course, Greeks have never been intimidated by forces larger than themselves. They dared to take on the Ottoman Empire in their fight for independence, in spite of little initial support from European powers. They invaded Turkey following World War I, going up against a country several times their own size. They said *Oxi!* (no)[9] to the Italians at the beginning of World War II, and they took it upon themselves to try to drive out the Germans occupying their country. Recently they went against the entire European Union in blockading Macedonia in open violation of EU decisions. It should come as no surprise that they would be impudent enough to take on the role of unsolicited adviser to the top manager.

Third, despite the participatory nature of most Greeks, they have a difficult time working together in teams. I was told by a Greek manager that one Greek can do the work of ten Japanese, but ten Greeks can't do the work of one Japanese.[10] Although we in the United States also have a strong individualistic and competitive drive, the value of teamwork is instilled within us as children as we participate in sports and work together in clubs. In organizations, teamwork combined with this competitive drive is espoused as the key to unlocking individual potential and for promoting an increased sense of ownership. As such, it is actively fostered by managers and supervisors. The optimum situation for managers is when employees can cooperate with one another to achieve team goals. Unfortunately, this situation rarely occurs in Greece, unless the team happens to be the family. Even sports teams in Greece are plagued by lack of teamwork and rarely live up to their potential. On the other hand, many managers believe that Greeks are fully capable of effective teamwork but have been prevented from cooperating by the typical Greek management style, which is highly centralized. My own experience in working with problem-solving groups in Greece suggests that there is much potential for promoting strong teamwork if the appropriate structures are put in place and a suitable atmosphere established.

Fourth, Greeks are naturally argumentative and will almost always offer a contrary opinion to what is said. This manifested itself even during my interviews with Greek managers. I would often bring up a point raised in another interview in order to test its reliability. Almost invariably, the person I was interviewing would dispute the point and give me his own version of the situation. Interestingly, as we continued our discussion there would come a place in the interview where, almost without fail, he would make the same point he had earlier disputed. I soon learned that the intent of the initial disagreement was to offer an alternative perspective, even if he agreed with what was said. Only in this manner, Greeks feel, can ideas and opinions be tested, all sides examined.

Management Style

The strong role of individualism and egalitarianism in the Greek work environment means that the field of management has not become established as a profession in Greece in the same way that it has in the United States. In fact, there is no word for "manager" in the Greek language. The term most often used is *diefthintis*, which translates as "director." Indeed, many managers carry out their jobs with a much more directive and controlling approach than is commonly found in Western companies. There is little delegation of responsibility involving real authority in Greek companies. It is not common to share information about the company with employees, since their access to this knowledge might restrict the power of the top managers. Few organizations use executive recruitment services, but rather choose their own employees, who are most often related to the manager in some way. According to Gordon Ball, a management consultant who has lived and worked in Greece for thirty years, hiring a relative gives the manager much more control over the employee. He uses the word "patriarchal" to describe the Greek management style.[11] Greek managers sometimes use the term *nikokyris* to describe their job, which means that they see themselves as the head of the family, the one who takes care of family matters. One manager spoke with pride in telling me that fifty-five of the one hundred thirty-five employees have been with the company for over seventeen years and that there have been no strikes against the company in its twenty-five-year history.

Seldom, however, does the directive style of the manager translate into harsh treatment of the employees. Since Greeks tend to look to their managers somewhat as a father figure, they expect the manager to take care of their needs as they arise. Almost all the Greek managers I interviewed told me that their employees are constantly coming to them with requests for favors, perhaps for time off because a brother is getting married, or sometimes to ask for money to buy an appliance for a new bride, or in some cases to request the use of the company car to pick up a guest coming from abroad. Most managers seem to feel an obligation to help out whenever they can. It is impossible, they say, to treat everyone impartially, and therefore the successful manager must be willing to put forth a great deal of effort to develop a personal relationship with his or her employees, becoming sensitive to their individual needs.

As indicated by the opening example to this chapter, the personal relationship with employees is perhaps the most important aspect of successful management in Greece. In company after company, I found that the essence of the effective manager's job lay in developing and maintaining personal connections with both subordinates and colleagues.

In an interview with the manager of a Greek packaging company, I was told that employees like to feel the manager near them. "Your coat and hat must be in the office," he told me, meaning that you cannot come in late in the morning and go for long lunches; your employees want to see you working hard.

A friend of mine has been reconstructing his father's house in a small village in the Mani region of Greece. Although the village is five hours away from Athens, where my friend resides, he found it necessary to be with his workmen during the day while they were constructing his house. "If you stay with them, providing *parea* [company] and kouvenda," he told me, "they feel like working and they take the same kind of care they would if it were their own house. If you leave them to work alone, they feel like slaves doing the work of someone else, and they are not likely to work very hard or with very good results."

In spite of the emphasis on personal relationships, managers in Greece are less likely to give verbal positive feedback to their workers than managers in the United States. There are several different reasons for such an omission. Greeks in general are careful about giving compliments because of the widespread belief in the "evil eye." It is thought that flattery and praise might bring bad luck to the person receiving it. Since people expect you to do a job correctly, there is no need to say something unless it is not done properly. Some managers are afraid that the employee will become too satisfied with him- or herself and stop working as hard if praised. Finally, there is a feeling that positive feedback might serve to lower the standing of the managers who give it or affect their ability to control their workers. Of course, it is inappropriate to suggest that praise should never be given. In fact, successful managers are good at encouraging their workers without overdoing it. As put by one manager, "To motivate a Greek all it takes is a couple of *bravos* and you will see them run very fast. If you don't, then it means they don't have any ignition."

Another aspect of management style that may appear inconsistent with the emphasis on personal relationships is the failure of most managers to use a team approach to organizing work. Most likely, this can be attributed to the long tradition of directive control from the top and the corresponding fear of losing control if responsibility is given to work groups. However, some managers are beginning to assign tasks to teams, and they are enthusiastic about the results. Although Greeks generally have difficulty cooperating with one another, it appears that, under the appropriate circumstances, the desire for involvement can override their contentiousness. One manager testified, "By establishing decision-making groups, much of the former criticism and complaining has been eliminated, because people were involved in the decision." In recent years there has been an increase in the number of seminars offered in Greece on quality circles and other programs that promote group work. Perhaps one contribution the manager from the United States can make to the Greek work environment is the encouragement of more teamwork and greater employee involvement in the decision-making process.

When it comes to motivating employees, Greeks have, as discussed in chapter 4, a strong sense of philotimo, or personal honor, and care must be taken not to offend it. If employees feel personally insulted, they can be extremely uncooperative and at times may take actions that serve no purpose other than to cause trouble. Just as the Greek who was granted a wish asked for God to kill his neighbor's donkey rather than ask for his own donkey, so Greeks seem to devote a lot of effort to harming their competitors rather than building up their own capabilities and resources.

In Homer's *Odyssey*, when Odysseus had successfully escaped from the cave of the Cyclops, rather than sail safely away, he taunted the blinded giant. In the process Odysseus not only barely escaped having his ship destroyed by boulders thrown at him by the Cyclops, he also revealed his identity—

which brought down on him the wrath of Poseidon, the Cyclops' father, and resulted in many dangers for himself and his men. To a large extent, his later troubles resulted from the short-lived pleasure that he took from getting back at his former captors. This tendency to think in terms of harming one's competitor, often at the expense of one's own self-interest, was illustrated during a visit to court that I made with a lawyer friend who was presenting a case for her client. The client was bringing suit against a tenant to evict him from a rented apartment. The defendant introduced evidence at the trial that would have made the court appearance unnecessary if matters had been known beforehand (in this case, the defendant presented evidence that the apartment was used for business, in which case he could not be evicted under the current law). Why did the defendant wait for the trial in order to present this evidence rather than settle it out of court? It seemed to me that it was motivated by his desire to cause trouble or embarrassment for the plaintiff. This was done in spite of the expense that could have been avoided by both sides had the case not been taken to court. Presumably, the reward for such behavior is the personal satisfaction one gets from seeing one's opponent suffer.

It is not possible to suggest to the foreign manager that he or she adopt a particular style of supervision when in Greece. Obviously, there are many styles of management, and what is appropriate in one company may fail in another. Like most supervisors in Greece, who do not study management as an academic subject, it is likely that as a foreigner, you too will have to develop your own management style the hard way—on the job.

Time Orientation

The Greek approach to time is considerably different from that found in the United States. One manager told me that Greeks approach a personal or organizational project the way one would a long road trip. You slow down at times and you speed up at times, depending on the conditions, and you can't usually predict what traffic or road conditions will be like. This often means that there is little advance planning of the type usually found in the United States unless it is imposed from the outside. The president of a small college (which is based on the American educational system but with Greek faculty and students) told me that when he first came to Greece from the United States, he gave an initial address to the faculty in which he discussed his plans for the future and presented them with an outline of his five-year program. He remembers the sinking feeling he had when he looked out and saw eyes glazing over and people looking bored, and when total silence greeted him as he finished the presentation. He later concluded that he was asking them to look too far into the future, which was much too uncertain to subject to a five-year plan. On several occasions I have asked friends what they have in mind for their lives in five or ten years. In most cases I receive an answer similar to, "Who knows? I may not even be alive then."

Others have told me that it is impossible to raise money for a project that has not yet started or a building that is not nearly finished. Something tangible must exist before anyone will have faith in its viability. The same is true for daily planning. When I work on projects with Greek colleagues, for example, I usually find that supplies are not ordered until after they give out, so there is always a delay between the time something is needed and the arrival of the new shipment. Once I called the airport to confirm that my departure flight was still scheduled for the same day, and in response to my question, the agent answered, "If it comes [from New York], it will depart."

Many of us who grew up in the United States have learned to plan our lives to maximize the use of our time and "get the most from life." For example, when we travel abroad, we may map out our itinerary by the day, if not by the hour. Before we leave home, we have often decided what we want to see, how long it will take us to get there, and how long we want to spend in each place. From the Greek point of view, such an approach may not be wise. Greeks might say that either we have amazing powers of prediction, or else we are extremely arrogant. There are so many "unexpecteds" that are likely to occur in a foreign land that it is impossible to stay with a strict schedule. We are likely to find more frustration than fulfillment in trying to follow an hour-by-hour or even day-by-day plan. This is particularly true if you happen to be visiting Greece, where either the taxis, buses, ferryboats, post offices, or telephone companies may be on strike; where traffic jams can cause hours of delay; where opening hours for the places you want to visit can change from those printed in the guidebook; where an unexpected celebration has closed all the schools and shops; where friends that you expected to meet have been called away.

One aspect of time management that will be noticed almost immediately by the foreigner is the ability of most Greeks to deal with several items simultaneously and to cope well with constant interruptions. Because the thinking process of Greeks is nonlinear, there doesn't seem to be a need, such as we have in the West, to complete tasks in a serial manner. Several people might be in the manager's office at the same time, each with a different concern, or the manager might be on two phones, concurrently working on various tasks at different stages of completion, all the while receiving and passing messages to the secretary or giving directives to other employees. The manager coming from the United States is more likely to need a great deal of uninterrupted working time and will tend to prioritize tasks and work on them one by one. This may be impossible to arrange in a Greek office, and even if you are successful in establishing such a routine, the distance it creates between you and your Greek colleagues and subordinates is likely to be detrimental. At the same time, it will be necessary for most Western managers to create some kind of private space for focused work. The key is to find a balanced combination of the open door and the personal retreat.

Making and keeping appointments in Greece is not an easy task. Generally, there is a more relaxed attitude toward the time of appointments, since everyone is aware of the difficulty involved in getting from one place to another in Athens as well as other large cities. Traffic jams, problems in hailing a taxi, the lack of specific bus schedules, and other difficulties make it impossible to predict when one will arrive somewhere. Moreover, the inconvenience and unreliability of the telephone system make it hard to call in case of delays. However, many managers are now accustomed to following the Western practice regarding appointments, and they will expect you to arrive at the time that was set. This is particularly true if you are a foreigner or if you have arranged to meet at some place other than the person's office. Of course, no one likes to be kept waiting, so it is best to specify whether or not the time of the appointment is flexible.

For many Greeks the rhythm of work revolves around the numerous times during the year when employees get away from their jobs. For most, it is the requirements of family and social obligations that take them away, but the opportunity is also viewed as a *dialimma*, or a break in the routine. Greece has a number of religious and state holidays, and whenever possible most people will take an extra day off in order to make a long weekend over which they can take their family to the countryside or their village home. When national elections are held, people turn the Sunday voting day into a four-day weekend, since, as said before, the majority keep their voting registration in distant villages and must travel there to cast their ballots. During the Orthodox Easter (which usually falls at a different time than the Western Easter) there is a two-week period during which schools are closed, and many people take off from work to take their children outside the city. In recent years the Christmas/New Year period, not traditionally as important as in the West, has also become an extended holiday interlude. It is impossible to do business in August, when practically the whole of Greece goes on vacation, and the summer in general is not a good time to count on finding someone in the office. Weddings, feast days, baptisms, and other celebrations provide additional opportunities for a dialimma. A tremendous amount of energy is expended in Greece to gear up for these breaks and then to recover from the long trip home.

In general, the passing of time in Greece is not viewed with the same sense of urgency or loss that is usually felt in the United States. As one manager told me, "How can you expect to set strict time frames in a country where a watch is worn for decoration?" (He has ten watches that he changes to match the suit he is wearing.) Seldom are people reminded to use their time wisely or to make sure every minute counts. It is considered more important to pass the time pleasantly and in good company and to enjoy every moment. This does not mean that Greeks necessarily waste time. However, it does point to the need for a different approach to scheduling and a different set of expectations for project deadlines. In Greece, it is more effective to emphasize quality than it is to try to force conformity to preset schedules. Above all, keep in mind that life moves to a different rhythm than it does in the United States, and the only way to function effectively in the Greek work environment is to get in sync with this rhythm.

Efficiency and Productivity

Greece has a reputation throughout Europe and other Western countries for having an inefficient business environment with low productivity. Although there are aspects of the general work environment that contribute to this perception, much of it stems from the notorious public sector. Greek civil servants receive nothing but condemnation throughout Greece, and the bureaucracy itself can frustrate the most determined individual. It doesn't take long to conclude that there is an adversarial relationship between the state and the people. Greeks have come to believe that those employed in government jobs are there to do whatever they can to make life difficult for the rest of the population. Since most companies must deal with the government bureaucracy in one way or another, it is important to plan for the extra time it will take to arrange all the paperwork that may be necessary for doing business in Greece.

Outside the public sector, which is often inefficient and rarely praised in other countries, there are cultural attitudes that contribute to lower efficiency in Greece than in more industrialized countries.[12] Most companies do not have organizational charts or job descriptions, and those that do usually ignore them. Greeks frequently have two jobs, and the demands of one job often cut into the requirements of the other. Rarely do Greeks work overtime, during lunch, or through breaks. Efficiency is never a conscious end; one rarely hears someone tell another to hurry up and finish the project. It is common to hear the word *arpakola* used to describe the way someone works, meaning that he or she completes jobs in a slapdash, sloppy manner because problems have been allowed to slide until something had to be done very quickly, leaving insufficient time for proper attention to how it is done or to the consequences of a hasty performance. A word sometimes used, especially by those who have served in the military, is *loufa*, which means to lie low or to keep mum and implies that one is trying to avoid assignment of duties.

Another drain on productivity is the way in which the working day is currently broken up. Although attempts are being made to adopt the standard European working day, most shops and services are typically open from 8:30 A.M.- 1:30 P.M. Monday through Saturday and then again from 5:00-8:00 P.M. in the evening on Tuesday, Thursday, and Friday. Starting up and winding down the day two times a day, three days a week takes away from productive work time. It also means that many people actually go to and from their jobs as many as nine times per week. In places such as Athens, where the traffic is so congested, the time and frustration involved in commuting siphons much energy from one's work.

Although Greek managers share the belief with their Western counterparts that humans must struggle against nature in order to survive, they do not share the Western sense of personal responsibility for the consequences of one's efforts. In Greece, failure is typically attributed to fate, although sometimes the situation gets the blame. As a preface to most efforts, Greeks may say *An theli o Theos,* or "God willing." You will often hear the phrase *Ti na kanoume?* or "What can we do?" The effort-optimism outlook so characteristic of the West, especially the United States, which assumes that anything can be accomplished through detailed planning and hard work, is not held by most Greeks. The tendency to shrug off poor performance is illustrated by a story related to me by a well-known music critic about the poor quality of musical performances of works by Greek composers. When criticized for their lack of preparation and inattention to various aspects of the musical pieces, the conductors replied, *Mi thigete ta kakos kimena,* or "Don't talk about the bad situation." They were implying that the job they were doing may not have been a good one, but at least something is being done. In other words, "Don't complain about my work, since without it nothing at all would be done."

One aspect of the work environment that bothers foreign managers is the occurrence of a great deal of seemingly nonwork-related activity in the office. Greeks love to tell stories and relate jokes, and they spend a great deal of time on the job chatting idly with each other. Several managers assured me that although Greeks may seem to be goofing off by engaging in such talk, they will usually make up the time "lost" as they continue working. The joking and storytelling are forms of stimulation and ways of promoting good relationships within the workplace. A similar explanation is often given for other activities that seem unrelated to the job at hand. One manager explained his willingness to allow workers to leave the office during the work day for personal errands this way: "The worst thing I could do is to say no to my secretary when she asks to go shopping in the morning. If I tell her to go in the afternoon after work, she will spend the whole day discussing why I didn't allow her to go, and she will do no work."

Outwardly at least, the Greeks give the appearance of a somewhat unproductive, inefficient workforce. If this attribution is in some ways accurate, it is still wise to interpret it with an eye toward its cultural and practical roots. As Greeks who have gone abroad have shown so many times, they can be extremely creative, ambitious, and hardworking when they work within a system that encourages and supports individual initiative. The task of the manager in Greece is to do whatever is possible to create such conditions within the company. If this can be accomplished, the image that currently plagues Greece might be somewhat alleviated. It is best to keep in mind, however, that there are aspects of the bureaucracy in Greece that will frustrate the foreign manager and make it easy to give up the quest for efficiency.

Approach to Rules and Regulations

Recently, a manager described to me the difficulty he was having making arrangements for a business transaction that involved bringing in materials from abroad. There were legal complications and high taxes that could make the project financially unviable. Upon hearing his story, I remarked that doing business in Greece must be frustrating. "Don't worry," he told me, "I'll find a window." This phrase and its sister expression, "I'll go through the window," are used by Greeks to indicate that, if the normal entrance is blocked, they will find a way through some other opening. A way can always be found around restrictive regulations.

One of my friends told me that breaking the rules is a Greek national pastime, and people take pride in being able to get around the law. Even worse, he said, people often brag about their illegal actions. This is quite evident in the payment of income taxes. Since the self-employed professional can hide income much more easily than a salaried worker, most professionals are experts at it. Recent statistics show that the average reported income for professionals is extremely low, resulting in the payment of very few taxes. For example, the average reported salary for full-time lawyers in 1993 was just over US $7,000, which is less than the average salary of a low-level government clerk and half as much as the average Greek factory worker. Nearly 60 percent of sales taxes go uncollected by the government, and the black market economy in Greece is worth $30 to $45 billion a year, as much as 40 percent of all economic activity.[13] Tax evasion is depriving the state of a sum amounting to about 10 percent of the current official national income. Some of my friends have told me that cheating the state has become a way of life, and statistics back up their claim; with only ten million inhabitants, Greece has close to eight million unsettled tax cases. To cheat successfully is the whole point of the game. There is even competition in who can cheat the most or the most innovatively. This attitude is rationalized as follows: The government officials are all thieves; why give them more to steal?

It appears to the outsider that Greeks tend to view rules as measures that are made to be defied. One writer puts it in the following manner:

> Volatile and unquenchably argumentative, the Greeks devote themselves with endearing openness to outwitting authority on principle even—or especially—when it wields a heavy truncheon; for, as we have seen already, they are apt to take most unkindly to anyone among themselves who sets himself up (or is set up by others) as their superior.[14]

Even laws that are created for the benefit of the individual are usually challenged. In the early part of the 1990s, the Greek government started enforcing a law that requires motorcyclists to wear a helmet, and police actually started stopping drivers and ticketing them for failure to obey the law. But the law was successfully challenged by motorcyclists carrying a helmet with them and "wearing" it on an elbow. They were able to argue that the law only specifies that the helmet must be worn, it does not say *where* it is to be worn!

A recent incident illustrates the defiance with which Greeks approach the imposition of new rules. In the spring of 1994 the parliament passed a law that required nightclubs to close at 2:30 A.M. on weekdays and 3:30 A.M. on weekends. There was growing concern that the performance of young people in school and the productivity of workers was declining because too many people were staying out most of the night. Of course, the club owners were upset with this new law because of its likely effect on their profits, but the outcry against the law came primarily from the general public. On the first night of the closings, there was a spontaneous gathering in Syntagma Square, in front of the parliament building, at 2:30 A.M. At this gathering someone erected speakers and put on music, creating a giant outdoor nightclub, continuing until 5:30 A.M., the normal closing time of the establishments. This soon became a regular event, and it attracted thousands of people each night. I once took a taxi from Athens around 1:00 A.M. and asked the driver if his day's work was finished and he was going home. He replied, "Going home? Of course not, I'm heading back to Syntagma Square for the party!" The subject of the closing of the nightclubs occupied the attention (and energy) of the nation for over two months. I am sure that the vast majority of Greeks were not affected by the "early" closings of the clubs, but they found it insulting that the government would try to take away their personal freedom.

This inclination to fight against limitations on personal freedom must be acknowledged and respected by managers in their development of company regulations. In order to gain adherence rather than spark rebellion, care must be taken to generate and present rules and regulations in such a way that they do not appear restrictive. Much time can be lost in fighting those who resist rules, and much resentment can be built up toward managers who are seen as strict rule enforcers. In several of my discussions with successful Greek managers, it was suggested that company measures be developed as much as possible with extensive employee involvement. While this is not always possible and does not guarantee success, it is important to do what one can to avoid the negative impact restrictive regulations can have on Greeks.

Getting Things Done

Since social relationships play an essential role in almost every aspect of the work environment, it should come as no surprise that personal connections form the backbone of Greek business. Without such connections it is impossible to accomplish anything, either within the government bureaucracy or in working with other organizations. Unless you know someone, there is little chance for getting a job, for advancement within the system, for obtaining information, or for success in the achievement of one's goals. I have known researchers who came away from Greece completely empty-handed, simply because they did not have the contacts that are necessary to get appointments, gain access to private collections, or help locate the desired information. The same has happened with organizational and governmental representatives expecting instant access to necessary information.

Holden suggests that Greeks treat bureaucracies much as they do religious concepts, both of which are abstractions. Just as human saints serve as the means of embodying an ineffable God, so do individual connections serve as the way of personifying cold and indifferent procedures and policies. Because Greeks tend to be warm and gregarious, the subjective is favored over the objective, and institutional channels are avoided in favor of personal contacts. Just as saints allow access to an unknowable higher power, a personalized approach to business opens up channels of communication within a system that might otherwise be impossible to penetrate.

The personal nature of work in Greece is manifested in two related but somewhat different ways. Politics in particular operates through a system of patronage that is based on *rousfeti*, a word of Arabic origin and with a Turkish history that means, roughly, "personal influence" and results in the dispensing of favors to supporters. Almost no politician is elected without the alliances formed through rousfeti, and it replaces many of the official procedures of government. It has been described as the oil that lubricates the system. As one senior member of the government said, "In Greece public employment has always been done by patronage. Government grants and public works projects have been given to friends."[15] Traditionally, it has been through rousfeti that jobs were arranged for relatives, admission to special schools was secured for the children of supporters, red tape was quickly cut for those to whom a favor was owed, and roads and schools were built in isolated communities of party MPs.

With changing economic conditions and after several government attempts to weaken it, the patron-client relationship is no longer so strong, but the age-old pattern of patronage continues to persist in one form or another. Today, appeals are still heard from and often granted to supporters who have a particular need. Of course, the Greek political system is not unique in the dispersal of personal favors and use of pork-barrel funding, but there are those who believe that the case of Greece is special because politics rarely seems to be about anything else. It is important to note that rousfeti is different from bribery, graft, or corruption (although this also occurs), which only serves to satisfy material desires. Rousfeti, on the other hand, serves to connect individuals, families, and clans in a complex web of relationships that some believe helps mitigate the otherwise extreme effects of individualism.

The other manner in which personal interdependence operates in Greece is through *meson*, referring to the contacts or connections that help one work through, around, or behind the system. You will hear people say "I would like to work with that company, but I don't have any meson," or "He didn't have any difficulty getting the permit, because he has meson," or "Without meson you will never get the appointments you are trying to set up." Despite the warmth and gregariousness of its people, in many ways Greece is a closed society that foreigners in particular have a difficult time penetrating on their own, and personal contacts become a necessity in order to get anything accomplished. Meson springs from contacts within the family, which was the primary social institution prior to contemporary times. Since Greece is a small country and opportunities are limited, meson still operates strongly.

Of course, in any country it is necessary to have contacts to accomplish tasks, but in Greece contacts tend to be more personal in nature. As one manager observed: "In the U.S. you use meson, only it is called a placement service. In Greece, the placement service is simply more human and there are no forms to fill out." There is no way, he told me, that you can prove your abilities to someone directly, so meson is the vehicle you use. This helps the company as well as the individual. The person who guarantees for you, the *mesazon*, knows you as a human being, just as the one who arranges a marriage knows you, so the company is more likely to get someone who will be loyal. Meson can only get you the job, however, and afterward it is up to you to perform well. If you do, then the status of the person who has helped you is enhanced, but at the same time there is an obligation created to assist if things don't work out. He told me that if one of his secretaries is not performing well, he will not fire her. Instead, he expects her to recognize the situation and to find a way to leave, perhaps by contacting the mesazon who initially recommended her. In this way, meson can provide for a way out as well as a way in.

To the foreigner, it may sometimes seem that the Greek work environment places so many obstacles in the path of getting things done that it is impossible to function effectively in the country. Indeed, some organizations have simply thrown up their hands in despair and decided that it is not worth their investment to set up operations in Greece. Certainly, there are many political, bureaucratic, and cultural impediments to working in Greece, but there are ways to deal with these barriers. The key lies in developing the personal contacts that can help open doors or can provide assistance in working through the maze of complications that exist. For the manager coming from the United States, "business as usual" will almost certainly fail in Greece, but with sufficient investment in establishing personal connections, doors can be opened.

Advice to the Foreign Manager

In my discussions with managers and consultants, I asked for their advice to those coming from abroad to work in Greece. I talked with Greek managers of Greek companies, Greeks who managed local offices of European companies, and managers and consultants from the United States or Europe who were working in Greece. All of them had seen the well-intentioned efforts of many foreign managers either backfire or fail to have their intended effect. They stressed that the business environment in Greece is not an easy one, and that foreigners should expect to do business differently. The following bits of wisdom are offered as tips for the foreign manager.

Don't let what is on paper fool you. Some organizations can show you organizational charts, mission statements, job descriptions, and perhaps even five-year plans. In only a few cases, however, do these have any real meaning. Most were created only for the sake of appearances and will not be implemented. Operating as a family business in an uncertain economy within a political system that is constantly establishing new rules and regulations makes whatever is put on paper of little value. These written depictions of organizational aims, even if they were developed with the best of intentions, are not likely to be given serious consideration by people whose lives revolve around personal and social considerations rather than abstract and impersonal descriptions.

Don't take everything at face value. Whenever I asked Greek managers to tell me about the characteristics of U.S. managers with whom they found it difficult to work, I never received anything more than a general response, and most people stated that there were no particular problems. Even if I brought up characteristics of Americans that I knew irritated Greeks, the response was usually that this only happens in a few cases and is not the general rule. "Of all the people we work with," they told me over and over, "Americans are the easiest to get along with." They were, however, always willing to tell me their criticisms of European managers, and when I interviewed British and Scandinavian managers, they all told me that Greeks often criticize Americans. It soon became clear that the Greek managers were trying to please me, to make me feel comfortable, to keep me from feeling offended. One manager suggested that because they spent so many years as subjects of the Ottoman Empire, during which time they had to be careful about what they said, Greeks are reluctant to express criticism of the manager (although they usually feel free to disagree with ideas, offer opinions, or give advice, as discussed previously). This may be especially true if the manager is foreign, and it may be compounded if they like the person a great deal. In this case they will want to please the manager, to make him or her feel satisfied with how things are going. Only when the manager becomes part of the ingroup can genuine feedback be expected. One consultant described Greeks as great dissemblers, meaning that they are very good at altering or disguising the appearance of something so as to conceal or deceive. There is no malicious or ill intent; they want you to be comfortable, so they tell you what they believe you want to hear. This often results in making the situation appear better than it actually is. For most managers from the United States or Europe, this "drives the frustration index off the chart," to put it in the words of the consultant.

Don't expect rapid change. Not long ago I had dinner in the home of Fred Gearing, a social anthropologist from the United States who now lives in a village in the Mani region of Greece. He discussed with me his 1962 study of the village, at which time all businesses were family owned. There were no partnerships, and the few that had been tried had quickly fallen apart. These attitudes also affected the bureaucracy, which operated on the basis of patron-client relationships. In 1994, after more than thirty years, Gearing felt the situation had not changed. At the time of my visit, he was conducting a follow-up study, and though the village itself had grown and prospered over the years, the businesses were still family owned and the bureaucracy functioned according to the same principles. It was a totally different business environment, but the way of doing business had remained unchanged by the forces that have been transforming the village from a sleepy isolated hamlet by the sea to a bustling tourist town. It remains to be seen if the cultural invasion taking place because of Greece's entry into the European market will bring about a different approach to the work environment in Greece, but change is likely to come slowly.

Don't create distance between yourself and your employees. "Greeks cannot accept someone wielding control from a high post" was the warning one manager gave me. Another asserted that it is impossible for a technocrat to run a company in Greece by issuing directives from above. Probably the two things that Greeks detest the most, especially in foreigners, are arrogance and detachment. Using a tone of voice or treating workers in a way that conveys a feeling of superiority will lead to resentment and the immediate creation of a wall between employees and the manager. Staying aloof will prevent active involvement in the work of the company and will lead to low motivation. This means that managers need to maintain an open door and genuinely welcome input and ideas. As expressed by one manager, "If you sincerely ask for ideas, soon they will be coming to you free of charge." It is not advisable to ask for formal (especially written) reports from employees, since these tend to be too impersonal. Informal face-to-face discussions apparently work best. One manager cautioned that even pretentious living can get in the way of good relations with employees. They want to see you as a good family person like themselves, going to church, taking good care of your children, and so forth.

Spend time with your employees. Greeks cannot work productively if they feel the manager is just a person doing a job, without any human feelings. Managers have to spend time learning about employees' families and their problems, expressing concern when there is an accident, illness, or death in the family. It helps to learn about their children, house, and perhaps their garden. The top manager of one company, whose plant is located two hours outside of Athens but whose main office is in the city, told me that he spends at least one full day each week in the plant, just visiting the employees and learning about their concerns and problems. He estimates that overall he invests 65 percent of his energy in the human affairs of the organization, even though his primary responsibility is to keep the company financially viable by managing the budget, working with suppliers and customers, and seeking new markets for the company's products. Another manager told me that you should "worry more about the people than about the product, because the people will take care of the product if they feel involved."

Pull, don't push. In order to motivate employees to put effort into a project, it is necessary to appeal to philotimo, which one manager described as the "turbo of the Greek's engine." When you "touch his philotimo," he told me, the person will put forth extra effort. There are a number of ways of doing this, he said, such as demonstrating one's own sense of personal honor or putting forth extra effort oneself when the time calls for it. He went on to describe a situation in which he had accepted a difficult project (for the government of Saudi Arabia) while forgetting that he had promised his employees two weeks' vacation over Christmas. He called an assembly of the workers in the plant and told them his situation and asked for their help. By suggesting that they should show the Saudis that the Greeks could pull it off, he appealed to the element of their philotimo that concerns national pride, and they all agreed to work the extra time without overtime pay in order to complete the project. Several managers and consultants stressed that you must find ways to entice your employees, so that they feel good about working harder and so that they feel they are helping themselves by putting forth extra effort. This might partially justify the allowance of nonwork-related activity on the job, since it can create a greater sense of loyalty and a sense of obligation to assist when circumstances require a special push to complete a project. One consultant advised that when people are giving you trouble, you must be especially kind to them so that they will feel a pressure to help you. "You stroke, you don't slap," he said. "It doesn't need to be excessive, just a bit of kindness. If you create an adversarial relationship, you're dead; if you are genuine and treat them like human beings, you are going against the norm and usually take them by surprise. If you charm the troublemakers, they almost always respond positively. Small things can go a long way."

Display competence and decisiveness. Employees want to see the manager as someone who is strong, decisive, and capable. "If you are just a nice person, you won't get anywhere," I was informed. The good manager needs a combination of strength and concern, and it is better to be decisive even if the decision turns out to be wrong. The foreign manager, especially, will be expected to be an expert, but if you are weak or fail to display competence, it will be difficult for the Greeks to take you seriously, and they may come to resent you. You might hear the expression *Stou kasidi to kefali egine ki aftos varveres*, which translates as "He became a barber on the head of someone with few hairs." This implies that one doesn't want to be the guinea pig for another's learning; that is, don't use my head in order to learn how to cut hair. No one wants to be a victim of another's inexperience, and Greeks are less likely than most to accept such a situation with understanding and patience. One manager suggested that managing in Greece is the "ideal test of one's own personality; you are directing people who believe internally that they are capable of doing your job better than you can, and you are being tested from the first moment. You must prove yourself from the beginning."

Demonstrate enthusiasm for your own job. Greeks use the word *meraki* to mean doing something with pleasure. If you don't have meraki for your work as manager, you will not succeed. Perhaps more so than in other countries, passion and zeal are contagious and help put others in the right mood for working. Of course, meraki must be genuine or else the employees will see through it immediately and will feel manipulated and perhaps insulted. On the other hand, if your employees see that you take delight in what you do and derive satisfaction from good work, they are likely to join with you in working together toward a successful outcome. Work in Greece is like the *tsamikos* folk dance, in which several people join hands and move in a line behind a leader, who performs a series of difficult and bold steps (often wheeling and leaping high into the air, turning midair somersaults, and in various ways giving stylized evidence of his bravery, his physical skill, and his courage) while holding on to a handkerchief held by a partner. If the lead dancer inspires the others with his or her enthusiasm and skill, they will respond and follow the person fully and perhaps become inspired to take their turn leading. But if the leader becomes lackadaisical about the performance of his or her role, the dance will quickly break down.

Finding the Right Management Style

The many differences that exist between the work environment in Greece and that in Europe and the United States do not mean that the outsider should adopt Greek attitudes toward work, try to function according to Greek management style, or try to mimic the patronage system found in Greece. In fact, several of those whom I interviewed warned against just such actions as these. The manager coming from abroad is expected to be different, and there is no way you can "out-Greek the Greeks." It is advisable to play your natural role, albeit with sensitivity to the cultural differences that exist in the Greek work environment.

At the same time, it is important to avoid trying to impose your own management style on the Greek work situation. When U.S. managers go abroad to live and work, they are usually highly motivated, eager to work hard, and anxious to accomplish a lot quickly. Certainly these are laudable characteristics, and they hold the key to success in many work situations. At the same time, these attitudes can make it more difficult to function effectively within the Greek work environment. Many foreign managers respond to their situation by trying to impose a different work ethic on the Greeks. This invariably meets with resistance and resentment. It is better not to fight the system; instead, find ways to work in harmony with the existing process.

It will take some time and will require a great deal of patience and openness to define a comfortable and workable mode of operation for yourself. Gradually, however, you will find that some of the patterns of the Greek work environment are very practical and necessary, and you may find yourself changed in subtle ways. Additionally, as your colleagues and subordinates come to know and accept you as part of their world, you will most certainly leave a mark of your own on the Greek way of working.

---

[1] Lee, *Freedom and Culture*, 151.

[2] It is more likely, however, that as a foreigner you will be asked about the nature of your work much sooner than will other Greeks. This occurs because some of the normal ways of establishing a connection, such as asking about your family or your home, do not have as much meaning. If you are living there rather than coming as a tourist, they are also curious about what brings you to Greece.

[3] In spite of the apparent contradiction, the individualism and independence of Greeks coexist with the strong loyalty and obligation to family and ingroup that were discussed in chapters 3 and 4. From one point of view, personal sacrifice for appropriate others can be a way of asserting one's own independence and promoting one's own ends. Laurie Kain Hart (see *Time, Religion, and Social Experience*, 172) says that individuality (idiosyncrasy of character and personality) is greatly admired, whereas autonomy that flouts family and community is condemned.

[4] Fermor, *Mani*, 206.

[5] *Economist* (22 May 1993): 18.

[6] Greece has a workforce of about four million people, of whom only 1.3 million are private sector employees, compared to just under 1.8 million employers and self-employed people. In 1988 only 130 establishments had more than 500 staff, but there were over 450,000 establishments with four staff or fewer. From Gordon Ball, "Personnel Management in Greece: The Spartan Profession," *Personnel Management* (September 1992).

[7] From *Greece, A Country Study*, xxix.

[8] Holden, *Greece without Columns*, 86.

[9] The official response of the Greek leader to the Italian ultimatum has been shortened to the single Greek word *oxi*, or "no." Each year on the twenty-eighth of October this day is celebrated as a national holiday known as "Oxi Day."

[10] This was not meant as a slap at the Japanese (any other national group with a reputation for industriousness could be substituted).

[11] Ball, "Personnel Management in Greece."

[12] In English, *efficiency* means producing the best result consistent with the effort put forth. It has connotations of a quality job, with minimum effort, in the shortest time. Several Greek terms are used for *efficiency*, but it is not clear that any single term captures the full meaning of the term in English. *Ikanos* is related to the word for "satisfied" and means "capable" or "competent." *Drastirios* is related to "activity" and means "energetic" or "hardworking." *Apodotikos*, which refers to "results," is most closely related to the English term and means "productivity" or "profit."

[13] Marlise Simons, "Athens Tries to Get Greeks to Own Up and Pay," *International Herald Tribune*, 26 May 1995, 5.

[14] Holden, *Greece without Columns*, 86.

[15] "Power on the Wane," *Time* (29 May 1995): 21.

6

Images of the Other

Intercultural experiences offer many rewards to those who approach their encounters with openness and a willingness to learn. Not only does one's own knowledge of others expand, but it is perhaps the best place to learn about oneself. One evening after a long discussion about the expressiveness and intensity of Greek communication style, I asked my friend to tell me how my wife and I appeared to him when we were conversing with each other. He hesitated at first, as if he were debating how to tell me the bad news, but after a moment he disclosed to me that we seemed to be constantly engaged in confidential business transactions. Surprised by his answer, I suddenly realized how serious-minded I must seem to Greeks and how utterly boring I must be as a conversation partner! Although I had spent years trying to decipher Greek culture, I now began to see how the Greek culture understood me.

Complementing this learning experience was an event that occurred a few months later, when I asked a friend to review a paper I was writing on the Greek approach to interpersonal conflict. In his response, he wrote that he found it both interesting and accurate, and that he was most struck by the way in which it allowed him to see aspects of his own behavior that he had never before reflected upon. Perhaps, he told me, such a description of one's culture by a foreigner serves as a mirror in which one can see oneself better. His comment concurs with communication theories that suggest that relationships serve as a "looking glass" for individuals to understand how others see them. Intercultural situations provide a unique opportunity, and one of the most significant gifts that Greeks and foreign visitors can exchange is the mirror that each can hold for the other.

Greek Images of Americans[1]

In spite of the ease with which Greeks generally express their opinions, I have found most people hesitant to give their views of Americans, especially if what they want to say is not favorable and they are talking with someone from the United States. I suspect that this reluctance is partly one of sensitivity to the feelings of the American. Fortunately, however, I have been able to listen to numerous conversations among Greeks about Americans who visit or live in Greece, and some of my friends have shared with me both the difficulties they have experienced with and the regard they hold for Americans. In addition, I have observed the behavior of my American compatriots and how the Greeks perceive their actions and comments.

To varying degrees, one's view of individuals from another country is inevitably linked to political considerations. For example, during the hostage crisis with Iran in the late 1970s, most of the U.S. public formed very negative impressions of Iranians, which were promoted by statements from the U.S. government about that country and its people. At that time I was responsible for developing cross-cultural learning programs at my university, and it was difficult to find students or families who would even consider hosting an Iranian student. Though they had no personal adverse experiences with Iranians, their disgust at the hostage taking was enough to make them hold unfavorable images of any Iranian. In the case of

Greece, we don't hear much in the U.S. news about its foreign policy or its politics. Greeks, on the other hand, are confronted daily with statements about U.S. actions around the world and the effects on their country. This undoubtedly affects the impression that Greeks form of Americans and presents an initial barrier that must be overcome.

While there have always been vast differences in how Greeks view the United States, many people, particularly those of the older generation with conservative political views, hold *Ameriki* in relatively high esteem. American philanthropy provided food, clothing, medical supplies, and financial assistance to refugees from the exchange of populations in 1922, and the U.S. military played a key role in the evacuation of Greeks from Smyrna as the Kemalist forces closed in on the city.[2] The financial and technical aid provided by the Truman Doctrine in the 1950s was critical to Greece in its struggle to recover from a decade of foreign occupation and civil war. In this century, a considerable number of Greeks have made their fortunes in the United States and sent large sums of money back to families in Greece. Many of these expatriates eventually returned to their country. Finally, conservative governments from 1974 to 1980 stressed cooperation with the United States and other Western powers.

Others, however, view the United States as a big bully, solving its problems with bombs and coercion. Much of the American aid following the Second World War was channeled into military objectives rather than used for economic development, and Greece's dependence on foreign aid made it essentially a client state of the United States. Few major military, economic, or political decisions could be made without American approval.[3] The military junta of 1967 is viewed by most Greeks as a result of American intervention, and many citizens were brutally treated by U.S.-trained military police. More recently, the U.S. handling of Iraq during the 1990 Gulf War made no sense to the Greeks. The bombing of

Libya when it refused to hand over suspects in the Pam Am bombing in 1990 appalled them. Greeks resent U.S. actions toward their country, such as Reagan's allegations regarding security deficiencies at the Athens airport. Lax security, Reagan claimed, allowed weapons to be smuggled onto the plane that was hijacked over Greece in June of 1985 by Lebanese members of the Shi'ite Hezbollah group. The loss of tourists brought on by the U.S. State Department's travel advisory cost the Greeks an estimated $400 million. Finally, Greeks feel betrayed by U.S. decisions regarding the Balkans following the breakup of Yugoslavia, especially those related to Macedonia. No one can understand the perceived U.S. support for the Muslim population of Bosnia rather than the Christian Serbs, since the Greeks are convinced that Turkey still has territorial ambitions and wants to reestablish the old Ottoman Empire.

Although my Greek friends assure me that they clearly separate how they feel about U.S. actions abroad from their estimation of individual Americans, these negative views form the background against which Americans are initially judged. Nevertheless, for most Greeks it is the personal relationship that counts, and they can be intensely anti-American politically and yet genuinely friendly and hospitable to individual Americans.

Unfavorable perceptions of Americans

Although it is difficult to make general statements, Greeks have trouble understanding or accepting many things about Americans. Most of them stem from basic cultural differences between the two groups, though some can be attributed to contextual factors. The primary context in which Americans are seen by Greeks, of course, is as newcomers in a strange land. Being strangers, Americans will naturally feel lost and will appear ignorant and helpless, since they don't know their way around the new culture. Just as it is easy for foreigners to appear "dumb" while in the United States, Americans don't always create a good impression while in Greece.

Naiveté. Greeks associate positive images with someone who is crafty, cunning, and guileful. Those who are most clever are the ones who rise to the top in politics and business. Greeks perceive Americans as naive, unnecessarily trusting, and sometimes gullible. They are easy to tease and it is simple to take advantage of them. Greeks have seen Americans pay too much for taxis, meals, gifts, rooms, and holiday packages. In the Greek view, Americans apologize too hastily, offer thanks too often, and say excuse me too easily. It is not hard to play on their sympathies, and they believe what you are telling them without sufficient examination.

Lack of knowledge of world events. Greeks love to discuss what is going on in the world at any given time, and they tend to keep up to date with the latest news through television, radio, or afternoon discussions at the kafenion. They tend to be as well informed about events in the United States as are most Americans, and they are especially aware of events and trends in Europe. The well-educated, even those in technical fields, are familiar with important works in literature and the arts, and they have a good grounding in world history. The educational system in the United States, as well as the news media, is much less global in its coverage, and Americans are simply unfamiliar with some of the key figures and events in world affairs. Greeks feel they are unable to carry on an intellectual discussion with most Americans under these circumstances, or they feel that if they are going to have a good discussion, they will have to spend too much time educating Americans.

Failure to participate fully in Greek social events. As said before, Greeks socialize constantly, and most people spend a lot of time attending celebrations and ceremonies involving friends and relatives. These events usually continue until late in the evening, although most people must leave early for work the next morning and children must go to school. In addition, there are many impromptu social events that develop as friends drop by or call at the last minute to suggest a movie or simply a drive to the sea. These occasions require a lot of one's time, and sometimes even my Greek friends complain about having so many social obligations. For most Americans, such a social schedule is too demanding, and too much socializing is viewed as an inefficient use of time. Greeks are disappointed when they invite their American friends to join them and the invitation is repeatedly declined. It sends a message that the American doesn't want to be in their company.

Inability to enjoy life. Greeks tend to savor those moments in life that bring pleasure to the senses. They cannot understand how Americans can devote themselves totally to work, especially if it involves reports, budgets, correspondence, and other noninteractive tasks. The Greek word for recreation is *psyhagogia*, which means literally "education for the soul." What is the purpose, my friends ask me, of working so hard if there are no moments left to enjoy the fruits of your labor? Greeks express their bewilderment at the degree to which Americans devote themselves to their work while neglecting their family and their own need for refreshing the soul.

Unrealistic expectations. While there is no assumption that foreigners will become Greek, visitors are expected to make the attempt to adjust their expectations and behavior to the country. Greeks often complain that Americans expect everything to be "like home," that they make too few attempts to adapt to their new environment. They criticize the Greek attitude toward time schedules, the paucity of expected services, and the lack of basic technical equipment. Americans are used to more creature comforts in the United States and a greater range of choices in products, but they don't realize, or they are unable or unwilling to accept, that many of these conveniences are more difficult to obtain in Greece. The inability to adapt to the situation in Greece is taken as an affront and is considered discourteous.

Excessive rule consciousness. For much of the past, Greeks have found themselves under the rule of laws and regulations that were stifling to effective functioning. Life could be made workable only by finding ways to get around them. Today, the bureaucracy in Greece sometimes makes it impossible to carry out one's job. Facing this situation, Greeks have learned to regard rules with less than total respect. Americans, on the other hand, tend to be rule followers, at least in comparison to the Greeks, and when they work as managers in Greece, they attempt to standardize operations, emphasizing rule enforcement and expecting everyone to follow the letter of the law, all of which rubs Greeks the wrong way. At the college where I taught in Athens, the American provost attempted in vain to impose *Robert's Rules of Order* during faculty meetings, an action which brought resentment and constant attempts to subvert the rules.

Objectivity in personal relations. Because family and ingroup considerations are of high priority to Greeks, it is impossible to be objective in rewarding jobs, doing favors, handing out promotions, and providing assistance. Americans, on the other hand, tend to take such actions based on judgments of ability and accomplishments rather than on personal relationships. The concept of fairness is quite different in Greece than it is in the United States. There was once a student demonstration in Athens against new rules that attempted to prevent cheating on exams. The main complaint was that these new rules were unfair because they prevented the students from fulfilling their obligations to their friends. Americans' objectivity is often viewed as cold and uncaring, and they are criticized for failing to take care of their friends.

Nonexpressive personality. Greeks are some of the most unreserved, outgoing, and expressive people in the world. They generally don't hide their emotions, and they are good at reading even subtle cues in order to respond correctly to someone else's mood. Americans, in contrast, often keep their emotions to themselves and are careful about letting others see their feelings. This makes it difficult for Greeks to know what Americans are thinking, creating a kind of awkwardness in communication and making it difficult to establish close relationships.

Attractive qualities of Americans

It is easy to focus on the negative when discussing images we have of others. Such a focus is understandable, since the problems caused by incompatibility are always at the forefront of our daily interactions and must be confronted in order to deal with the people around us. However, it is important to remember that relationships would not be possible if the participants did not offer something positive to each other, and there are several aspects of American behavior that Greeks admire and hold in high regard.

Friendliness. It is not uncommon when walking down the street in almost any town or city in the United States to be greeted by complete strangers, who will smile and sometimes strike up a conversation. It is one of the few places in the world where there exists such an outward show of congeniality. Although they may be initially surprised and perhaps even baffled by such behavior, Greeks generally find such warmth refreshing. Greeks also find Americans courteous, and they appreciate their good manners, their kindness, and their willingness to be helpful when the occasion arises. In addition, Greeks find most Americans cheerful and optimistic.

Willingness to work hard. Americans hold a strong work ethic that is probably matched or surpassed only by the Germans, Swiss and Japanese. It is not uncommon for Americans, especially professionals, to devote most of their evenings and weekends to their jobs, even bringing work home or taking it with them on vacation. Unlike most Greeks, for Americans one's job is an important part of one's identity, and work itself is highly esteemed. Although Greeks don't understand how Americans can spend so much time working, they admire them for their dedication and commitment to their job. Greeks respect Americans for their accomplishments, both their technological achievements and their high standard of living, though they may sometimes be envious.

Ability to admit mistakes. One highly valued American character trait is the willingness to take personal responsibility for bad decisions or poorly executed tasks. As children, Americans are taught that it is a sign of strength to admit mistakes. Greeks, on the other hand, do not easily recognize or acknowledge that they have done something wrong. You will seldom hear an apology or admission of guilt. The American's willingness to say "It was my fault" or "I'm sorry" may sometimes be viewed as insincere, but it is generally admired by Greeks. They see it as a sign of courage and self-confidence.

Truthfulness. From a very young age Americans are taught to be honest in their dealings with others. The Biblical commandment given to Moses that prohibits "false witness against thy neighbor" is generalized to "Thou shalt not lie." Children are punished severely for not telling the truth, and many of our children's stories show the terrible consequences of misrepresenting the truth. Of course, with the corruption and behind-the-scenes dealings that have captured the news headlines in recent years, the image of the "honest Abe" American has been severely tainted. Nevertheless, Greeks perceive individual Americans as relatively straightforward and sincere. Most of the Greek managers I have talked with tell me that their dealings with Americans are so much easier than those with other Greeks or with Arabs, Russians, Bulgarians, and Western Europeans. They appreciate the Americans' straightforward, no-nonsense manner.

American Images of Greeks

The common image Americans have of Greeks is formed on the basis of very little information. Most do not personally know any Greeks, although they may have seen films or special television programs on Greece. For those who live in areas where there are substantial Greek populations, such as Chicago, New York, or Washington, D.C., there are opportunities to eat at Greek restaurants and attend Greek festivals. In these situations the opportunity to become acquainted with people of Greek ethnicity is limited. In addition, there are as many as one million U.S. citizens who travel to Greece each year as tourists. In this role they tend to meet primarily service personnel and others whose job it is to help them enjoy their stay (or at least spend their money while in the country). They pass most of their time in the company of other tourists and rarely have the opportunity to spend time with Greeks, other than those involved in the tourist industry.

The most meaningful images of Greeks come from U.S. citizens who come to Greece to live and work. The more extensive and in-depth contact that is likely to occur in this situation inevitably leads to both difficulties and rewards. Described below are some of the criticisms and compliments that Americans are likely to express during their stay in Greece. No one person living in Greece will find that all of these perceptions hold for him or her, but an awareness of the experiences of others can help one anticipate and understand the feelings one does have better.

Complaints about Greek culture and character

Given the ethnic diversity in the United States, there is little agreement among sociologists that an "American culture" exists about which general statements can be made. At the same time, it is commonly accepted that a set of mostly Western values and behavior patterns underlies political, governmental, educational, and media systems in the United States. Americans are exposed in their daily lives and at their jobs to a set of assumptions about the nature of privacy, the use of time, proper behavior in personal relationships, and appropriate forms of communication with others. These values often conflict with those in other countries, and Greece is no exception. These cultural differences lie at the base of difficulties Americans encounter in Greece.

Lack of privacy. The Greek language (both ancient and modern) has almost one million words and is a wonderfully expressive language. Yet it lacks a word for privacy. Not only is the word missing, but the concept itself makes little sense to most Greeks. Few people want to be left in solitude. Historically, solitude meant the lonely life of the shepherd or the fisherman, facing dangers of the mountains or the sea alone. In general, Greeks desire the company of others to a much greater extent than do Americans, who like to have quiet time in order to reflect. In their desire to see their guests happy, Greeks constantly invite Americans to join them on excursions, to have dinner together, to attend a festival, or simply to sit and talk. Sometimes Americans feel that they just want to be left alone to read a book, watch the sunset, or go for a stroll. In addition, Greeks often ask about matters that many Americans consider personal. Their inquisitiveness and desire to establish common ground lead to questions that Americans think are none of their business. In contrast, Greeks feel left out when their friends don't become concerned with their problems. Americans associate privacy with personal freedom, while Greeks associate privacy with isolation and exile.

Inefficient use of time. Traditionally, Greeks have not viewed time as a commodity that can be molded by human beings. *Na perasoume tin ora,* or "to pass the time," is a phrase that one hears often in Greece. There is great concern with filling the time in an interesting way, but the value of "saving time" is not part of their normal system of thought. Americans, on the other hand, see time as something that can be "accumulated," "used," or "budgeted." For the Greek, the clock is not a master, and the need to organize activities according to a strict schedule is distasteful, though it has become necessary in recent years with more contact with European organizations. Americans often see the clock as their friend, helping them get the most done and providing a means for coordinating their activities with others. For Americans, efficiency is an important concept that almost always carries positive connotations. Americans complain that Greeks are inefficient in their use of time. They arrive late for appointments, waste too much time socializing, and wait until the last minute to do things. Differences in the perception of time are constant sources of irritation and frustration for Americans.

Feeling of superiority. According to many writers and observers, the high opinion of themselves held by most Greeks (and the corresponding low opinion of others) has not changed since Homer's time, when, as noted earlier, Odysseus taunted the Cyclops, ignoring the pleas of his men to sail away to safety. It is common to hear Greeks talk about both daily events and international crises as if only their ideas have merit. A Greek's boasting most often takes the form of simple rhetorical "one-upmanship," but to many Americans it comes across as egotistical. Since Americans tend to value humility (even though it may not be widely practiced), the Greek's display of superiority is offensive and often leads an American to shun conversation or to admonish the speaker for overestimating him- or herself. The latter, of course, only serves to offend the host.

Reluctance to admit mistakes. Greeks generally see one's ability to accomplish tasks limited by circumstances not entirely under human control. Anthropologist Ernestine Friedl argues that self-esteem is maintained among Greeks by attributing failures to external conditions rather than to personal inadequacy. If something goes wrong, a person is likely to blame a lack of proper facilities or equipment, or to say simply *Pos na ksero ego?* or "How was I to know?"[4] By contrast, Americans believe that people have a great deal of control over their affairs, should always take personal responsibility for something that goes wrong, and then try to fix it. Harry Truman's "The buck stops here" is widely admired. When Greeks appear to feel no remorse for their wrongdoings,

Americans perceive them as stubborn and believe they are simply trying to avoid the negative consequences of failure.

Anti-American rhetoric. Throughout its modern history, Greece has suffered from interference in its internal affairs by outsiders. In some cases, this interference provided necessary aid (e.g., during the war for independence, the German occupation, and the rebuilding of Greece in the 1950s). However, more often than not, interventions have been motivated by strategic interests of outsiders and have not taken into account the needs and desires of Greece. During the past twenty-five years much of this interference has come from the United States, the nation on which Greece has been most dependent. As is the case in other parts of the world, this dependency is often the source of conflict, so it is not surprising that there are significant disagreements over U.S. foreign policy, particularly in regard to Cyprus and Turkey. Although one no longer hears strong public statements from officials against American policy, when the socialist government was in power from 1981 to 1989, it regularly criticized and condemned the United States. Such anti-American rhetoric is often reflected in everyday conversation, and Americans complain that this criticism of U.S. policy is excessive and unnecessary. I often hear this kind of statement: "Greeks feel unfairly treated, and they somehow expect me to be able to do something about it." Fortunately, Greeks rarely intend their negative comments about the United States to apply to individual Americans, but nevertheless it is difficult for most Americans to hear their country constantly criticized.

Sensitivity to criticism. One of my Greek friends, who has lived many years abroad, told me that while he criticized things about England while living there, he did so from a somewhat detached point of view. When he finds things wrong in his own country, however, he criticizes them with a passion because, he told me, he feels so deeply for Greece and wants to see things work better. As happens in other countries, Greeks offer sharp and sometimes stinging criticisms about other Greeks and about conditions in their country but become defensive and seem offended when foreigners criticize Greece even slightly. There are many factors involved in Greek sensitivity to criticism which Americans should be aware of. First, Greeks truly want their guests to enjoy their stay, and complaints tell the Greek that he or she has not done a sufficient job in extending hospitality. Second, Greeks see themselves as having a perspective on their history which is not likely to be shared by foreigners, and negative comments from outsiders are seen as superficial, even in cases when the Greek agrees with the foreigner. Finally, with their history of foreign intervention and domination, Greeks have had to bend often to the desires of others, and complaints may be seen as subtle hints that they should once again adapt to the wishes of the foreigner.

Subtlety in communication. One of the many apparent incongruities in Greek behavior is the frequent use of delicate cues to communicate messages. This occurs most often when they are trying to obtain some information that is not public, secure a favor, discourage some behavior, or discern the mood of others. Greeks are curious about others' affairs and secretive about their own, and to satisfy their curiosity, they become skilled in eliciting information by indirect means. In addition, because they like to please their friends and guests, they are constantly looking for cues that indicate how they can best satisfy them. Americans complain that it is sometimes difficult to tell what a Greek really means, and they are often surprised to receive things they did not ask for. Sometimes what is simply a question of curiosity for an American is taken as a hint that something is desired, and the Greek may go to great trouble to obtain that something for their guest. Although Greeks are straightforward and direct in most of their communication with others, Americans are likely to become confused by the elusive nature of many messages.

Disparaging remarks about minority groups. Greece is linguistically, religiously, and culturally homogeneous. With the exception of a small Muslim minority in the far northwest corner of the country, a few Gypsy communities, and the recent arrival of refugees from Albania, most Greeks have little experience with non-Anglo foreigners. The few contacts they have with individuals of African descent are likely to be the workers from Ethiopia who serve as maids or laborers. Disparaging remarks are often made about Africans, African Americans, Gypsies, Arabs, and Jews. Frequent negative reference is made to the *mavri*, or dark-skinned people of the world. U.S. society still has a long way to go before it fully breaks down racial barriers, but it is generally unacceptable to make disparaging remarks about African Americans, Latinos, Asians, and Native Americans, at least in public. Americans in general are more exposed to cultural diversity than are Greeks, and most Americans like to think of themselves as tolerant of differences in skin color and ethnic background. Many Americans feel that Greeks are prejudiced and perhaps even racist in their attitudes toward differences in skin color, and although few African Americans visit Greece as tourists or live there as residents, the experiences of those who do confirm this picture. Compounding the difficulty is the belief among Greeks that they are not prejudiced, and suggestions to the contrary may result in a strong defense of their tolerance and an equally strong condemnation of racism in the United States.

What Americans appreciate about Greeks

Gatherings of sojourners often dwell on complaints they have about the host country. While some venting of frustrations stemming from cross-cultural adjustment is healthy, the qualities of the host country that draw us toward it too easily get lost. Some of those attractive aspects of the Greek character and style that Americans comment on most often are the following.

Hospitality. Perhaps the most well-known Greek custom is their offer of philoxenia. As Fermor so aptly describes, philoxenia has an almost religious importance, based on "a genuine and deep-seated kindness, the feeling of pity and charity toward a stranger who is far from home (as in ancient Greek the word *stranger* and *guest* are synonymous)."[5] The invitation to sit for *kafedaki* (a small cup of coffee) or for ouzo, or sometimes to spend the evening with food, wine, and conversation gives many Americans the feeling of being treated like a god. Such kindness is viewed as both humane and practical—there are many stories of Greek gods traveling the countryside disguised as strangers. This warmth and welcome are experienced particularly by those who travel to the small villages that lie outside the well-trod paths of the tour buses or wander the sections of Athens less frequently overrun by tourists. Greek hospitality along with the accompanying welcome feeling is one of the primary reasons that many visitors hold such pleasant memories of their trip to Greece and hope to return as often as possible.

Generosity. Closely related to philoxenia but with far greater consequences is the overwhelming spirit of giving that accompanies true friendship in Greece. It is difficult to imagine that any people could be more unselfish and giving than Greeks. If they have a friend in need, they will part with everything they own, if necessary, to take care of their friend. Most Greeks I know are not possessive of their belongings, and if the occasion arises they lend them freely to me. They ask, "What is the use of having things if they can't be shared with others?" The American notion of accumulating material objects for personal enjoyment is much less common in Greece, in spite of the consumer mentality that has recently gripped Athens. They give of their time as well and help in any way they can to obtain information or make important contacts. As I worked on this book, my friends helped me locate materials, made arrangements for me to meet managers, constantly discussed the concepts about which I was writing, and gave me feedback on drafts of the chapters. They even offered me places to stay and a place to write. I have heard similar stories from other foreigners, and most are genuinely impressed by the generosity of the Greeks. Indeed, I have been touched by the kindness they have shown me, and it has helped me become more generous with my own possessions, time, and other resources.

Serendipity. It often seems that making plans is viewed by Greeks as a form of constraint, as an imposition on their sense of freedom. *Diathesi*, or mood, is an important factor in governing the daily events of life, and it would be viewed as a waste of time to engage in an activity when one is not in the mood just because it was planned earlier. At the same time, plans can change suddenly because something different comes along that had not been anticipated. In their social life, Greeks leave much to fate, and every day can be an adventure. Americans find this spontaneity refreshing, a welcome change from their normally overscheduled life in the United States.

Enthusiasm. Greeks have an unparalleled zest for life. Kazantzakis' Zorba may not be an accurate portrayal of the vast majority of Greeks, but he does represent an important aspect of the Greek spirit. When the author writes that Zorba "sees everything every day as if for the first time," he is describing the curiosity, the vitality, and the energy that most Greeks possess. Americans find this enthusiasm stimulating and energizing.

The Complexity of Images

My experience in Greece has taught me that images are much more complex than they first appear. When we describe others, we are doing more than simply stating facts or perceptions about the other. Although images tell us something about how one group sees another, they also teach us something about how groups think of themselves.

If we look behind the images we hold of Greeks, we can learn much about how we see ourselves. We often admire things in Greeks that we don't find in ourselves. We come to appreciate these characteristics of Greeks as we discover their benefits, and perhaps subconsciously we wish we could emulate these behaviors. The difficulties we find with Greeks may simply reflect aspects of our own society or of ourselves that we reject.

Because they often carry double meanings, images can be a significant source of learning. As you adjust to the people and culture of Greece, it is important to pay close attention to how you see others and how they see you. By examining your own images of Greeks, you can learn about yourself, and by examining Greeks' perceptions of Americans, it is possible to learn more about the Greeks. Although Greece is not a particularly easy place to find a mirror, the reflections that it holds can add to the treasures that you carry away from your cross-cultural adventure.

---

[1] Many people argue that the term *American* is most appropriately used to refer to all peoples of the Americas, both North and South, rather than just to residents of the United States. However, Greeks almost always use the term *Ameriki* when referring to the United States, and the most common term for a U.S. citizen is *Amerikanos* (for men) and *Amerikanida* (for a woman).

[2] See Louis P. Cassimatis, *American Influence in Greece, 1917-1929* (Kent State University Press, 1988).

[3] Clogg, *A Concise History of Greece*, 146.

[4] Friedl, *Vasilika*, 86.

[5] Fermor, *Mani*, 204.

7

Developing Positive Relationships

Almost anyone who listens to Greek popular music or watches
Greek dances is immediately caught up in the feelings and
moods they convey. There is something about the stirring
melodies and the stimulating pulse that touches the deepest
parts of the heart and soul. It is easy to become transported
into another world even without understanding the words of
the songs. However, learning to play the music or perform
the dances requires a great deal of practice and patience,
even for accomplished musicians and dancers. For those accustomed to the regular meters of Western music, it is extremely difficult to get in sync with the irregular patterns and
groupings of Greek rhythm. In a similar manner, the Greek
social world moves to an unfamiliar rhythm, and those who
try to enter it often feel strangely out of tune or off balance.[1]

The foreigner will find no simple way to join the dance of
the Greek social world, and no one will expect a non-Greek
to be able to take part fully. But anyone who enters the
interpersonal domain of Greek life with openness and a genuine desire to participate will discover a rich culture and warm
people with deep roots in a profoundly meaningful past. As a
first step, it is necessary to understand three key aspects of
social relations in Greece: company, mood, and talk.

The Company of Others

During our most recent extended stay in Greece, we were faced with the necessity of furnishing a bare apartment that we rented. As is common in Greece, the apartment came without stove, refrigerator, washing machine, and other standard appliances that we expect in the United States. Fortunately, we were able to borrow these things from people we knew. It was evening when we went to pick up one of the appliances that a friend had stored away years ago. After we had retrieved it from behind the stairs and tested its condition, we prepared to leave. As happens so often, we were not allowed to go until we had shared dinner with them. There was no invitation issued, and no one asked us if we would like to stay. They just started preparing dinner. Since we had arrived during the time of the evening meal, it was assumed that we would join them. It was obvious to us that they had not planned on eating much themselves that evening, since no food was already prepared. However, pots were immediately placed on the stove and food started coming out of the refrigerator. We protested, saying that there was no need to fix food for us, since we could easily stop on the way home and get something to eat. This resulted in incredulous looks of dismay, with the reply, "We're not worried about your going hungry. We want your parea."

In Greek society, a high value is placed on sociability. To be alone and to be bored are the two most dreaded states of existence for most Greeks. In a corresponding manner, to leave someone by him- or herself is the worst thing that you can do to a friend. Parea has intrinsic value and is considered essential for the well-being of a person. The individual who is outgoing and gregarious is approved of by others, while those who keep to themselves are considered *periergos*, or curiously strange.

Greeks believe that the most satisfying way to pass the time is in the company of friends. Talking together, sharing the events of the day, discussing the world's problems, and telling jokes provide a feeling of connectedness and unity. While in Greece, you will constantly be asked to provide parea for someone, or if you want parea for whatever activity you are about to pursue. For Americans this often presents a dilemma. It is reassuring to receive so many invitations to have dinner together, go to a movie, sit and have a coffee, go for a *volta* (stroll), or take a drive. Yet the constant interruptions and their often spontaneous nature make it difficult to stick to a planned schedule and can infringe upon one's need for private time. The offers of companionship can sometimes seem an intrusion rather than the intended show of concern. A linguist who teaches at the University of Athens told me that in Greek culture parea replaces privacy.[2]

In order to step into the Greek rhythm, you must learn to genuinely enjoy keeping company with others. Whenever possible, accept invitations to join your friends for activities and reciprocate by making efforts to include friends in your own activities. Though it will be difficult, it is usually necessary to give up much of your privacy. Time spent together with your Greek friends is of utmost importance in developing relationships. Being together shows that you value the relationship and find it satisfying to be in their presence. Just as important, it is from being with others that you learn about Greek culture. No amount of reading or study will replace the moments of insight that come from the spontaneous exchange of ideas while in the company of friends.

In the Right Mood

Very little happens in Greece unless the person has the right diathesi. While mood certainly affects everyone's performance anywhere, in Greece it is essential that one pay close attention to the mood of the person with whom one is conversing or working. I have discovered on many occasions that my requests for information are ignored or brushed off if the person is not in the mood to answer. Asking for a favor goes unheard if the mood is not appropriate. I often sense that certain discussion topics are inappropriate because the other person is not in the mood for a particular type of conversation. For example, during a recent Easter dinner I was rebuffed by my friend for trying to engage in serious discussion of political and environmental issues, when his mood was clearly one of forgetting all worries and concerns and just enjoying the moment. In work situations, requests for assistance are often ignored if the person is not in the right mood.[3] To be successful, one must carefully judge the mood of a person before issuing assignments or making requests.

There are two important concepts related to mood. First, Greeks frequently use the verb *varieme*, which translates roughly as "lacking enthusiasm" (literally, "to be bored"). It is common for Greeks to say "I am not enthusiastic about driving so far," or "I am not enthusiastic about staying here," or "I am not enthusiastic about doing my homework." For the Greek, to be "not enthusiastic about doing something" is a perfectly good reason not to do it. One doesn't fight against boredom but accepts it as a natural state of existence that comes often. In any case, it is assumed it will be difficult to do a good job under circumstances of boredom. For the Western mind, it is easy to see expressions of boredom as excuses and to attribute laziness to the person making such statements. Our strong emphasis on self-control, self-motivation, and discipline leads us to believe that we can overcome boredom and accomplish our tasks or goals in spite of our mood at the time. Greeks are much more likely to go with the flow of their feelings, and they will not often call on self-will to do things for which they clearly have no energy. From their point of view, anything done while not in the mood is not likely to lead to good results, so forcing oneself to do something one's heart is not in is not seen as a wise move.

A second concept that is closely tied to mood is *kefi*, a word of Arabic origin that plays an important role in daily life, especially in social events and celebrations. While it is difficult to translate this word directly, it generally means "high spirits," "enthusiasm," or "drive." Frequently heard expressions include, "I wanted to dance, but kefi didn't come" (I couldn't feel any enthusiasm); or "I don't have kefi today" (I am in low spirits); or "He is full of kefi for his work" (he is motivated).

When used in reference to celebratory occasions where there is feasting, dancing, music, and drinking, kefi signifies an altered state of being. An individual (usually male) may often dance alone, in sublime unselfconsciousness, providing his own variations to the music. Lost to his surroundings, his eyes closed or fixed on the floor, his arms often outstretched and fingers snapping, he moves trancelike within his own private world. He may be experiencing either melancholy or joy, but the transcendent feeling of kefi is an intensely personal sensation, and the dancing is a form of catharsis, or internal purification. No one applauds his dancing, although most may watch his performance. Everyone recognizes that he dances for himself and not for an audience, no matter how important his parea may have been in helping to induce the kefi.

A "pure" feeling of kefi is an intoxicated state, but it is not brought about by alcohol alone. Atmosphere or ambience is more important in creating kefi, including music, food, and the company of good friends. A critical component of kefi is the message in the songs that often triggers the transcendent state. The senses are assaulted with stories and well-known song lines that lead the listener into self-reflection. Almost all Greeks can easily identify with the sensuous melodies and touching themes of traditional and popular music, especially the music known as *rebetika*. One friend told me that when he listens to certain songs he hears his own story and his own life appears before him. Kefi is an expression of competing and often contradictory forces. It is a feeling that comes to individuals, although it most often comes in the company of others; it is the ultimate in self-expression, but it may create a similar mood in others; it can promote unity in a group, but it also sets individuals apart from it. Since kefi represents an escape from self-control and social constraint, on rare occasions kefi may be carried too far, with the person exhibiting behaviors that are unacceptable or saying things that could hurt others. In this case, kefi results in *dropi,* or shame, since the individual has stepped beyond the bounds of individual freedom allowed by kefi.

In the West, we subordinate feelings, believing we can manipulate them to our advantage. Greeks, on the other hand, view feelings as a controlling factor, able to influence strongly one's ability to perform and the quality of one's performance. Greeks are good at reading cues of others in order to understand if they are bored or if they have kefi, and they can suggest (or not) activities appropriate to the mood. It is not easy, of course, for them to read the mood of foreigners, because we convey different cues, and it is easy to attach the wrong meaning to them. In developing friendships and good working relationships with Greeks, it is important to be able to recognize the mood of the other person and adjust your communication accordingly. This requires careful monitoring and increased sensitivity to the other person. It is in discerning the mood of the other that subtlety in communication becomes an important asset. Greeks' ability to read delicate cues allows them to know when a person has the appropriate diathesi. It will take practice and patience to develop the ability to read and respond correctly to mood, but it is a key element in adjusting to the Greek rhythm.

Engaged in Dialogue

One of the most important words in the Greek vocabulary is *logos,* a term with a long history and numerous shades of meaning. For the ancient Greeks, *logos* meant both speech and reason, or logic. These two concepts were integrally linked in the mind of the Greek, because speech is what makes logic possible, thus separating humans from animals. In Greek philosophy, from Aristotle onward, it was also used to mean formative principle. There were pre-Christian, Greek-speaking Jewish philosophers (e.g., Philo of Alexandria) who linked the concept of logos with the wisdom of God. The Gospel of Saint John from the Christian New Testament, originally written in Greek, states, "In the beginning was *Logos*, and *Logos* was with [literally "toward," from the Greek *pros*] God, and *Logos* was God." There have been many sermons from Christian pulpits centered around this passage, although it is most usually translated as "Word." Among the concepts associated in contemporary Greece with logos are speech, reason, word, reckoning, proportion, relation, explanation, argument, story, the grammatical parts of speech, and language. To understand the many uses of logos is to decipher the essence of Greek communication.

Logos forms the root of the word *dialogos*, or dialogue, and this concept is central to every aspect of Greek life. As was noted earlier, more than in most societies, Greek children are given a great deal of verbal stimulation from an early age, for use of words is perhaps the most important skill they will learn. Speech acts as a stimulating force, serves a linking function, and plays an essential role in creativity. It is integral to entertainment, solving problems, and building trust and rapport. It helps to bolster self-esteem and provides an outlet for self-expression. Above all, it provides the means by which relationships are formed and developed. However, as discussed in chapter 4, Greek dialogue takes a different form from that heard among most Westerners. It is much more intense, more engaging, more inquiring, and generally more combative.

Moreover, Greeks identify different types of dialogue according to their purpose. At a workshop for Greeks on conflict-resolution skills I recently attended, the American trainers were trying to distinguish between the terms *dialogue* and *debate*, arguing that successful resolution of conflict requires more of the former and less of the latter. It was difficult for the trainers to explain the difference between these terms to the Greeks, since the language doesn't separate them very clearly. Greeks distinguish between kouvenda (casual conversation) and *syzitisi* (serious discussion), using the former term to denote talk that is used to pass the time or to keep company with one another and the latter term to indicate that the talk is more thoughtful and deals with more significant or more consequential topics. However, syzitisi is also translated as "debate," which for Greeks is synonymous with "serious discussion." Any dialogue aimed at conflict resolution must take place through debate. In the Greek mind, debate serves as a stimulus both to their own thinking and to the unfolding of the discussion. Nonevaluative listening is a concept with no practical use. Greeks expect to challenge and to be challenged.

In contrast to the United States, where politics is avoided as a topic in most social situations and where argumentative politics is virtually a taboo, the most common topic of debate in Greece is politics. Pericles, the great orator of ancient Greece, asserted, "We do not say that the man who takes no interest in politics is a man who minds his own business. We say that he has no business at all." This seems as true of present-day Greece as it did of ancient Athens. If you visit any taverna, kafenion, park, office, or home, you will almost always find people discussing political issues, and the debate is usually as intense as you would expect in the halls of the parliament. And given the fierce individualism of Greeks, every person has his or her own opinion on every issue. Their unbridled enthusiasm allows them to argue their point of view strongly without any pretense of looking at it from all sides. Newspapers also follow this pattern. Athens has the largest number of newspapers of any capital city in the world, and each of them is dedicated to a particular political point of view, characterized by biased and sometimes sensational reporting. Unbiased opinions are considered the sign of a weak mind that can't decide what to believe. One traveler has compared participants in political discussions to drivers in downtown Athens. He says that while most drivers are fully on the lookout for dangers and challenges from both sides and from the rear, they are oblivious to the possibility of head-on collisions.[4]

One of the reasons that debate does not have negative connotations for Greeks is that expressed emotions do not have the same effect as they do on most of us in the United States. When someone speaks to us in an angry tone, we take it personally, and we generally feel angry, upset, or hurt by the remarks. We may develop negative feelings toward the other person, perhaps even a grudge, and these can permanently affect our relationship. In Greece, the strong expression of emotions does not have this effect. I have seen on numerous occasions my friends becoming angry with one another and expressing this anger visibly, yet there seem to be no lingering hurt feelings. An hour later they are laughing and drinking beer together. In interacting with Greeks one must keep in mind that impassioned arguments do not mean lost friendships (and in fact usually appeal to and engage the Greeks).

In addition to discussions of politics, Greeks have a rich oral tradition in which storytelling and jokes play an important role. One writer suggested that humor "is as essential a spice to their conversation as oregano is to Greek food."[5] Greeks remember jokes easily and tell them endlessly, and I have sat several times with groups engaged in joke telling until the early hours of the morning. In villages old men will sit through the afternoon telling stories of their childhood to anyone who happens to be near. Of course, these stories usually become more grandiose, more significant, and more self-flattering than reality. They make much better stories that way, for both listener and teller!

To be a full participant in a discussion with friends allows a freedom of expression difficult to duplicate in U.S. society. It is important to point out, however, that Greeks can and do take offense at what someone may say to them, and when grudges develop there is little possibility of resuming normal communication. Indeed, it has been true until recent times that if arguments developed into vendettas, they affected entire families and were even passed from generation to generation. To an outsider, it is difficult to recognize the line between serious argument and insulting talk, but if something is said that touches the philotimo of the other person, then it is difficult to recover the relationship. One mistake that I have seen many foreigners make is trying to match moves with the Greeks in debates without understanding the difference between a remark that provokes and a remark that insults. It is advisable to err on the conservative side when you are not sure how far to go, since it is better that you be viewed as a boring conversationalist than it is to insult a friend.

Developing friendships and good working relationships with Greeks does not mean you have to become a good storyteller, a joke master, or a political zealot. It does mean that you must do a lot of listening, that you must not become disturbed by a great deal of debate, and that you must not take it personally when people disagree strongly with what you say. Ancient Greeks believed that the truth could only be discovered through dialogue. Lively conversation is what makes for good parea, and it is the primary ingredient in bringing kefi to a gathering.

Entering the Greek Social World

Although there are many motives for visiting Greece, everyone is faced with the dual challenges of cross-cultural adjustment and intercultural communication. In Greece, both are made easier by philoxenia, which makes the Greeks some of the best hosts in the world. The traditional offer of a place to sit, a glass of water, and a sweet is still practiced by many Greeks one meets in the countryside or along the streets of Athens or Thessaloniki. However, philoxenia is not experienced by every visiting foreigner, and for those fortunate enough to enjoy such a connection to the lives of their hosts, the "place to sit" does not necessarily translate to friendship.

As is the case for guests in any home, the key to a successful stay lies in the establishment of a personal relationship with your hosts. From the moment that hospitality is extended, foreigners are continually being judged by their attitudes and actions. The hosts are looking for signs of good character, expressions of genuine interest, and respect for the Greek way of life. It is not always easy to move beyond the acquaintance stage, but there will be many opportunities for developing long-lasting friendships. Although no shortcuts or guarantees of success can be offered, there are certain attitudes and efforts that facilitate the development of positive relationships. To enter the Greek social world, one must adopt a proper frame of mind, exhibit appropriate attitudes, actively participate in Greek social life, and make an attempt to learn the language.

A proper frame of mind

One of the keys to successful adjustment in a new culture is the recognition that you are a guest in another's home and not the owner of the place. *Evesthisia*, or sensitivity, is a word that evokes positive images for Greeks. Unfortunately, they find too many instances of insensitivity in guests from the United States. I have often heard the joke about the culturally insensitive traveler who, when quoted a price in another currency, asks: "How much is that in real money?" Once, while accompanying a friend from the United States while she completed her shopping in the Plaka district of Athens, I was shocked to hear her ask that question of the shopowner, who had just told her the price of a copper plate. The shopowner took great offense at this remark and gently asked her to find another place to buy her gifts, that he was unable to accept any of her "real money." I too was embarrassed and apologized to the man in the small store for the insensitivity of my friend. Remarks that belittle or put down aspects of Greek society and culture are offensive and can destroy any possibility of further communication.

One must also expect to be inconvenienced, frustrated, or taken advantage of from time to time. Everything will not go according to plan, and things will not be done as they were back home. People will not understand you, they will not know how difficult they are making your life, and they won't realize that sometimes you just want to be left alone. The tendency is to attribute these difficulties to the people and the culture that surrounds you, but you must realize that the source of such problems is within.

The tendency to blame the environment is strong, but it can create great difficulties in relating to others. For example, it is easy to become frustrated when you are trying to explain an idea or request or attempting to obtain something while communicating with someone who speaks English as a second (or third) language. When this happens, the tendency is to place blame on the other person. You wonder why they refuse to understand. It is important to keep in mind that it is your own inability to speak the other's language that is causing difficulties. Realizing this allows you to be appreciative of the efforts the other person is making to comprehend you and to feel grateful that you can be understood at all.

Appropriate attitudes

Inviting a person into their ingroup is not a casual step for Greeks. They realize that such a move requires a commitment of family resources and may demand sacrifice in certain situations. On the other hand, they also know that a new member brings many potential benefits. New friends help widen their own world of companions, providing company and bringing outside stimulation. Additional ingroup members increase prestige with friends, especially if the new member is from the United States, England, or another wealthy Western country. Finally, new relationships bring with them the possibility of future assistance in times of need or difficulty, of opening up educational or job opportunities, and of traveling abroad more easily—most Greeks prefer to travel to places where they have friends rather than visit a place just to see the sights.

In some ways, Greek philoxenia is a testing ground, allowing the host to probe for commonalities and providing the foreigner the chance to demonstrate the proper qualities that make a good friend. Greeks judge a person quickly and look for indications of certain attitudes that are required for the relationship to function smoothly. Most important, they need to see the visitor demonstrate respect, sincerity, and openness.

Respect is an attitude universally desired yet seldom demonstrated by foreigners. When in a strange environment, it is easy to point out what is wrong with the place one is visiting and to give advice about what should be done to make things better. Such advice is almost never welcomed, and in most cases it is not good advice anyway. To step into a new country and begin making suggestions for improvement after only a few days, months, or even years is insensitive and will not be appreciated, just as we as Americans take offense when foreign visitors offer unsolicited advice about how to improve things. Constant complaining carries with it a similar disregard for host feelings, as does the tendency to associate only with fellow sojourners. Instead, take note of the positive aspects of the people and the country, letting your hosts know the things about which you feel positive. In addition, take the time to learn about the history and the culture; then you can ask questions that will engage your host in stimulating conversation—nothing shows greater respect for people.

Sincerity is one of the simplest yet most difficult attitudes to demonstrate in an intercultural context. This is especially true in Greece, where people are quick to judge and where American tourists, in particular, may be viewed as superficial. Sincerity is a combination of desire and trust. First, you must be genuinely interested in sharing your opinion or in asking questions to help you learn. Unless your interest is genuine, Greeks, who are adept at discerning deceitfulness in others, will immediately dismiss you as just another smiling tourist. At the same time, communication must occur in the context of trust and rapport to be judged as sincere. Very seldom can these qualities be developed instantaneously. It will take patience, time, and energy to build a relationship that demonstrates sincerity. If your hosts see that you are committed to learning and willing to give of yourself, they will reciprocate.

Openness is not a quality that comes naturally, although it is essential for successful cross-cultural adaptation. The survival of most life-forms requires closing out most foreign substances lest the system be severely disrupted. Yet it is also the quality upon which growth and change depend. People find it easier to be open to differences when functioning in a familiar environment, since the safety of their surroundings provides the feeling that the system itself will hold together in spite of the entrance of unknown forces. When traveling or living in a new place, there is little safety in the surroundings, and there are so many challenges to the system that the survival mechanism is likely to close off all invaders from the outside. Yet it is precisely in the new environment that the greatest need for openness and the greatest potential for learning and growth exist. Greeks are impatient people, and if they do not detect an openness to learning new ways, it is unlikely that they will take the time to help you adapt to their culture.

Active participation in social events

Michael Sotirhos, a Greek American who served as U.S. ambassador to Greece from the summer of 1989 to January of 1993, created a positive impression among my friends, despite the fact that generally they are not enthusiastic about U.S. diplomats in Greece. He spoke Greek fluently, and because he used the language as if he were native-born, he favorably impressed large numbers of Greeks. The key to his success in generating good feelings, however, came from his active participation in Greek social events. Almost every day he was shown on television attending a wedding, a baptism, a funeral, a nameday celebration, a local church service, or a social gathering. People commented frequently about his activities, never failing to point out how unusual this was for a foreigner, especially a representative of the U.S. government.

Although you will not receive all the invitations issued to a U.S. ambassador, you should make a special effort to attend social gatherings. Of course, it is not appropriate to simply walk uninvited into a wedding party, but if you live and work around Greek people, you will be invited to people's homes, and you will be asked to join them in celebrations and festivities. While traveling, I have been invited to attend several village feast days simply by striking up a conversation during lunch at the village taverna. Greeks are naturally inclusive, and active participation in their activities comes easily and will bring many rewards.

While it is natural to turn to other Americans or foreign visitors in order to feel more at home instead of struggling to get along in the Greek community, it is important to resist this temptation. There are numerous groups in Athens and Thessaloniki composed of mostly U.S. citizens living in Greece, and there are other English-speaking organizations devoted to particular interests. I know people living in Greece who try to duplicate their life in the United States. It is easy to spend one's entire time in the company of fellow sojourners, missing out on the growth and personal satisfaction that come from interaction with your hosts. Of course, it can be beneficial to compare notes and share common experiences with one's compatriots, and from time to time it is psychologically necessary—and comforting—to talk with someone who speaks your language fluently and with whom you can share experiences about home. Try to keep in mind, though, that too much time spent in the comfort of familiar faces will deprive you of the essence of your stay in Greece.

Attempting to learn the language

The single most difficult but rewarding task a visitor to Greece can undertake is the study of the Greek language. It is difficult because of the unfamiliar alphabet, complicated grammar, extensive vocabulary, and constantly evolving nature of the language. The Greeks themselves consider their language very difficult for foreigners to learn, and they rarely expect the visitor to speak any Greek. Indeed, it is not necessary to know Greek for purposes of traveling, shopping, and taking care of daily chores. Although the majority of Greeks do not speak English fluently, there is always someone nearby who can translate, and most service establishments cater to English-speaking guests. The language of international business is English, and most people who deal directly with outsiders have studied abroad in England or the United States. Since Greece and Cyprus[6] are the only Greek-speaking countries in the world, with a combined population of less than eleven million, studying modern Greek might not seem to be a good investment of time for most people. Why put oneself through the agony of studying the language?

The most important reason to study Greek is that it enhances one's opportunities to meet and get to know Greek people. Perhaps nowhere in the world do people respond more positively to the outsider who tries to learn their language. Since Greeks have come to expect almost total ignorance of their language by visitors, the person who speaks even a few words and phrases of Greek is a pleasant surprise to them. The butchering of their language coming from the mouths of foreigners doesn't unduly distress Greeks, and they are genuinely pleased when guests put forth effort to learn it. The attempt to use Greek provides an indication that the visitor has taken his or her stay seriously. Greeks understand that a relationship with any foreigner will demand time and effort, and learning the language provides a strong indication that the guest is committed to the task.

In addition, the use of Greek demonstrates respect for an important aspect of Greek identity stretching over thousands of years. The Greek language contributed significantly to the evolution and growth of Christianity and the emergence of Europe from its Dark Ages. The development of modern scientific thought and Western philosophy is based on Greek. During the Hellenistic, Roman, and Byzantine periods, Greek was the international language, much as English is today. It contributed thousands of words to the vocabularies of English and other languages, and it forms the basis for most scientific and medical terminology. With such a rich history, it is only natural that Greeks are proud of their language.

A Spirit of Discovery

In Greek mythology there are numerous references to the Gates of Hades, where the boatman waits to ferry passengers across the river Styx into the next world. Generally, these gates are thought to exist at a place where the sea enters a steep cliff in a remote and inaccessible place. There are several remote areas in Greece where this mythical spot might be located, but one of the most likely candidates is the Mani region, deep in the Peloponnese. Local legend claims that the Gates of Hades lie along the coast of the rocky peninsula of Cape Matapan (Taenaron), south of the deserted village of Vathia, currently being restored by the National Tourist Organization. We once stayed in one of the old stone towers in Vathia with a friend whose roots are in the Mani, and on the spur of the moment we decided on a hot July day to try to find the Gates of Hades.

Of course, the site is not listed on any map, and most of our attempts to ask for information were met with nothing more than puzzled looks. Someone, however, directed us to the end of a rough, rocky road, where a shepherd pointed us up and over a hill covered with boulders and thorny bushes. He said that we would see a place on the other side of the hill where the sea disappeared into the cliffs between two black rocks. There was no trail, and once we reached the top, all we could see were more steep hillsides and a rough sea breaking on the cliffs. We were determined to find the gates, but it was not clear where we should go or how we would manage to get there if we could find them. The only thing that kept us from turning back was the fact that we had already come so far. Although we felt disoriented and afraid that we had lost our way, we searched in various directions, finally locating a place where the sea hit the cliffs yet produced no spray, indicating that the water must be flowing inside the cliffs. We climbed down with great difficulty, and to our satisfaction, there we found exactly what the shepherd had described. We enjoyed our lunch underneath a rock overhang on top of one of the "gates," watching the sea flow into the cave that opened between the two black rocks.

While there was nothing spectacularly scenic about the spot, and although we never met the legendary boatman asking for our drachma to carry us further, there was nevertheless a special feeling emanating from the site, and we were immensely pleased that we had persisted in our efforts even when we thought we were lost. On returning we decided to take a somewhat different route, and we were further rewarded by finding the remains of an unexcavated town built in ancient times around a quiet cove, where we found simple mosaics of dolphins on some of the floors of the ancient houses. The entire experience was one of meaningful discovery brought about by curiosity and a willingness to explore.

Similarly, very little of what I know about Greeks came from systematic study. Most of my significant learning experiences and lasting memories came from unplanned and unexpected events. Taking the wrong turn frequently led to unexpected discoveries, confusion often brought me unanticipated understanding, and following my intuition almost always resulted in unforeseen findings. I have learned that the nondeliberate path is the one that takes you beyond the ordinary. The best views are those that come from the precipitous places, and there are no gentle ascents to these special places.

To gain the most from your experience in Greece requires impromptu exploration and a corresponding willingness to lose your way physically, psychologically, and socially. The physical disorientation will often occur whether or not it is sought, since the streets of the cities and the roads of the countryside twist and turn to follow the contours of the land and are not well marked for outsiders. These unmarked roads and trails have led to many pleasant experiences similar to our lunch by the Gates of Hades.

The willingness to become lost while on a journey of discovery requires a sense of self-confidence in your ability to deal with situations as they arise. The unexpected is not always pleasant, and you may often find yourself in difficult circumstances or entangled with connections and obligations that you would rather avoid. If you have faith in your ability to "roll with the punches," however, you can join the ranks of those who have followed in the footsteps of Odysseus on a journey of discovery. Fortunately, there are no monsters to fear in Greece, and there are many people who will be pleased to help you find your way.

Words of Caution and Encouragement

The first chapter of this book cautioned the reader that it is impossible to capture the "Greek reality," since any sense of what is real must be experienced in context. Thus, this brief sketch of Greek values, beliefs, and communication patterns must be interpreted in light of the limitations that necessarily accompany such descriptions. My aim was not to achieve objectivity or completeness. Not only is it impossible to provide a comprehensive picture of Greek culture but also it should never be expected that any individual Greek will conform to the portrait provided in these pages. The situation is further complicated by the fact that no matter how much we learn about another culture, and no matter how much a particular person embodies the elements of that culture, the intercultural encounter is itself a unique event in which you will create a common meeting space that transcends both cultures. If this space can be filled with meaningful learning experiences, your exploration of the Greek mosaic will become a genuine expression of rich intercultural communication.

---

[1] For an excellent discussion of dance and culture in Greece, see Jane Cowan, *Dance and the Body Politic in Northern Greece* (Princeton, NJ: Princeton University Press, 1990).

[2] Personal communication from Vassiliki Nikiforos, Department of Linguistics, University of Athens.

[3] If a Greek sees that a friend is truly in need, however, this perception will trigger the mood that is necessary for providing assistance.

[4] Davenport, *Athens*.

[5] Gage, *Hellas*, 26-27.

[6] Cyprus is composed of both Greek-speaking and Turkish-speaking communities, and the official languages of Cyprus are Greek and Turkish.

Postscript

Ithaki, the beautiful piece by Constantinos Cavafy, became a source of inspiration for me during my writing of this book. Named after the island of Ithaca, which lies in the Ionian Sea in western Greece, *Ithaki* draws from Homer's *Odyssey*, in which Ithaca is the kingdom of Odysseus, to which he was returning after the long Trojan War. Although I had previously read the English translation, it was when I studied it in Greek that *Ithaki* captured my imagination and served as a catalyst for my thinking. Below is the full text of *Ithaki*, which two of my friends, Ioannes Kapelouzos and Rena Pappas, helped me translate from the original Greek.

> As you set out on your journey to Ithaki,
> wish the way to be long,
> full of adventures, full of discovery.
> Lastrigonians and Cyclopes,
> angry Poseidon do not fear,
> such you will never find on your way.
> As long as your thoughts are high,
> and well-chosen emotion touches your soul and body,
> The Lastrigonians and Cyclopes,
> and wild Poseidon you will not encounter,
> unless you carry them inside your soul,
> unless your soul erects them in front of you.

Wish your journey to be long.
Many summer mornings to have
when with what pleasure, with what joy
you enter harbors you're seeing for the first time.
May you stop at Phoenician trading posts,
and acquire fine things,
mother of pearl, coral, amber and ebony.
And sensual perfumes of every kind,
as many sensual perfumes as you are able.
To many Egyptian cities you should go,
to learn continuously from the learned ones.

Always on your mind have Ithaki.
The arrival there is your destination.
But don't hurry your trip at all.
It is better many years to take
and, old, eventually to settle on the island,
rich with what you have gained on the way,
not expecting Ithaki to give you riches.

Ithaki gave you the beautiful journey,
without her you wouldn't have set out on the way.
Other things it doesn't have to give you any longer.

And if poor you find her, Ithaki didn't fool you.
So wise you have become, with so much experience,
you will have understood already
what is the meaning of these Ithakis.

—Constantinos Cavafy

Glossary

Listed below in alphabetical order are the Greek words and phrases used in the text, with a brief description for each.

acropolis [ακρόπολη]: the high point of the city, where a citadel was usually built. The Acropolis of Athens is the site of the Parthenon.

afentiko [αφεντικό]: the word often used for "boss." Literally, the word means "master" and, while it is sometimes used by workers as an endearing term for their boss, it has its roots in the master-slave relationship.

agonia [αγωνία]: anxiety, agony, or suspense.

agora [αγορά]: public space; marketplace.

Amerikanos [Αμερικανός] (for a man) and *Amerikanida* [Αμερικανίδα] (for a woman): used to refer to a citizen of the United States.

Ameriki [Αμερική]: term most often used to refer to the United States of America.

an theli o Theos [αν θέλει ο Θεός]: "God willing."

andartes [αντάρτες]: guerrilla fighters.

apodotikos [αποδοτικός]: efficient, profitable.

arpakola [αρπακόλα]: used to describe the way someone works, meaning that one completes jobs in a slapdash, sloppy manner because one lets problems slide until something has to be done

151

very quickly without proper attention to how it is done or to the consequences that will result.

atomo [ἄτομο]: the word for "person." It comes from the word for "atom," which was believed by ancient Greek scientists to be the indivisible unit of the universe.

Catastrophe [Καταστροφή]: the Asia Minor disaster of 1922, when the Greek forces were defeated by the Turks. Thousands were killed, and over a million Asia Minor Greeks became refugees, forced to resettle in Greece.

cosmos [κόσμος]: cosmos, universe, earth, world, people, circles, society.

dialimma [διάλειμμα]: a break in the routine; interlude; intermission.

dialogos [διάλογος]: dialogue.

diathesi [διάθεση]: mood, disposition.

diefthintis [διεθυντής]: the word used for "manager." It translates as "director."

dimotiki [δημοτική]: demotic or spoken Greek.

doulia [δουλειά]: a word for "work" (i.e., What work do you do?). It is closely related to "slavery" and "bondage."

drachma [δραχμή]: the Greek monetary unit.

drastirios [δραστήριος]: related to "activity" and means "energetic" or "hardworking."

dropi [ντροπή]: shame, shyness, or modesty.

eleftheria [ελευθερία]: freedom.

Ellada [Ελλάδα]: Greece, Hellas.

enosis [ένωση]: union. This word was the slogan used by Greek Cypriot nationalists, when they were fighting for independence from Great Britain from 1955-1960, to denote their desire for union with Greece.

ergasia [εργασία]: workmanship, craftsmanship; one's occupation, profession, or trade. It also can be used to refer to a work of art.

evesthisia [ευαισθησία]: sensitivity (to another's feelings, mood, or way of life).

grammatia [γραμμάτια]: literally, promissory notes or mortgages. It was often used in villages to refer to young brides.

iconostasi [εικονοστάσι]: a shelf on which icons and other sacred objects are kept as part of the family altar. It is also used to refer to the large icon screen found in churches.

ikanos [ικανός]: capable or competent. It comes from *ikanopio* [ικανοπιώ], "to satisfy."

ikoyenia [οικογένεια]: family.

kafedaki [καφεδάκι]: a small cup of coffee.

kafenion [καφενείο]: coffee shop; a gathering place for men, traditionally off-limits to women; a core institution in Greek society.

kalokeri [καλοκαίρι]: summer.

Kalitera na se misoun para na se lipounde [Καλύτερα να σε μισούν παρά να σε λυπούνται]: "It is better to be hated than to be pitied."

kandili [καντήλι]: a hanging oil lamp.

kefi [κέφι]: a word of Arabic origin that generally means high spirits, enthusiasm, or drive.

koumbaros [κουμπάρος]: godfather of one's child or the best man at a wedding.

kouvenda [κουβέντα]: conversation.

logos [λόγος]: speech, word, reason (or logic).

loufa [λούφα]: to lie low, to keep mum; used in the military to imply that one is trying to avoid assignment of duties.

mavri [μαύροι]: dark-skinned people of the world.

Megali Idea [Μεγάλη Ιδέα]: the "Great Idea," the aspiration to unite all areas of Greek settlement into a single state, with Constantinople as the capital.

meraki [μεράκι]: enthusiasm; doing something with pleasure; a labor of love.

mesazon [μεσάζον]: the person who guarantees for you; the go-between, intermediary, middleman.

meson [μέσον]: pull, influence, power. It refers to the contacts that help one work through, around, or behind the system.

mezedes [μεζέδες]: tidbits, snacks; usually consisting of several small plates of appetizers (cheese, sausage, fish, olives, tomato, etc.) to accompany a drink, often *ouzo*.

Mi thigete ta kakos kimena [Μη θίγετε τα κακός κείμενα]: "Don't talk about the bad situation." It implies that one should not worry that the job is not being done correctly, since at least something is being done.

Min tous mathenis na se perimenoun [Μην τους μαθαίνεις να σε περιμένουν]: "Don't let them become accustomed to expecting you back at a certain time." It is sometimes used by men to imply that one should not be tied down by the wife's expectation that you will return home at a certain time.

mythistorema [μυθιστόρημα]: a novel combining myth and history.

na perasoume tin ora [να περάσουμε την ώρα]: to pass the time; implies a concern to fill the hours in an interesting way.

nikokyris [νοικοκύρης]: landlord, owner, master. May be used by a manager to describe his job, which means that he sees himself as the head of the family, the one who takes care of family matters.

ouzo [ούζο]: the aniseed-flavored spirit that is made by distilling the residue of the wine process. It is a popular aperitif served with *mezedes* at sidewalk cafes, particularly during the hot summer months.

oxi [όχι]: no.

palevoume [παλεύουμε]: "We are struggling."

parea [παρέα]: the company of friends.

patrida [πατρίδα]: country, home, fatherland, birthplace.

pedomazoma [παιδομάζομα]: child gathering; sometimes called the "janissary levy." It was the most feared obligation of the Christians during Ottoman rule, when every village was required to send its most handsome and intelligent children to serve as elite soldiers in a special unit of the Ottoman army or as bureaucrats in the government.

perasmena, ksehasmena [περασμένα ξεχασμένα]: "What is past is forgotten." Let bygones be bygones.

periergos [περίεργος]: curious, strange.

philotimo [φιλότιμο]: dignity, self-esteem, sense of honor, moral worth; literally "love of honor." There is no adequate translation into other languages.

philoxenia [φιλοξενία]: kindness to strangers or hospitality.

pisma [πείσμα]: stubbornness.

poniros [πονηρός]: clever, crafty, cunning.

Pos na ksero ego? [Πώς να ξέρω εγώ?]: "How was I to know?"

prika [προίκα]: dowry.

psemata [ψέματα]: lies.

psyhagogia [ψυχαγωγία]: recreation, amusement, diversion, entertainment; literally "education for the soul."

rebetika [ρεμπέτικα]: a musical tradition that developed in Aegean port cities and came to be associated with the Asia Minor refugees.

rousfeti [ρουσφέτι]: reciprocal dispensation of favors; a word of Arabic origin with a Turkish history that has traditionally "oiled the wheels of society."

Stou kasidi to kefali egine ki aftos varveres [Οτου κασίδι το κεφάλι έγινε κι' αυτός βαρβέρες]: "He became a barber on the head of someone with few hairs." It implies that one doesn't want to be the guinea pig for another's learning; that is, don't use my head in order to learn how to cut hair.

syllogi [σύλλογοι]: social clubs.

synennoisis [συνεννόηση]: a common understanding and ability to come to agreements.

syntrophos [σύντροφος]: a companion or comrade; often used by older married couples to refer to their mate.

syzitisi [συζήτηση]: serious discussion; can also mean conversation, debate, argument, controversy.

taverna [ταβέρνα]: restaurant. In the cities or tourist areas, some tavernas have music and/or floor shows.

tavli [τάβλι]: backgammon.

Thelis na mou foresis foustania? [Θέλεις να μου φορέσεις φουστάνια?]: "Do you want me to wear a dress?" It may be used by a man asked to work in the kitchen or do housework.

Thelo na ime afentiko tou eaftou mou [Θέλω να είμαι αφεντικό του εαυτού μου]: "I want to be my own boss."

Ti na kanoume? [τι να κάνουμε?]: "What can we do?"

tsamikos [τσάμικος]: a folk dance in which several people join hands and move in a line behind a leader, who performs a series of difficult and bold steps while holding on to a handkerchief held by a partner.

Varia ine ta ksena [βαριά είναι τα ξένα]: "Heavy are the foreign lands." It is the first line of a well-known song about living abroad.

varieme [βαριέμαι]: to get tired of, or not feel like doing something; translates roughly as "lacking enthusiasm" (literally, "to be bored").

volta [βόλτα]: stroll, walk, or outing by car.

xenitia [ξενιτιά]: sojourning in foreign lands on either a permanent or temporary basis; the state of being abroad or "in exile" from one's home.

yiayia [γιαγιά]: grandmother.

yitonia [γειτονιά]: small neighborhood or vicinity.

The following system of transliteration from modern Greek to English is used:

α : a

β : v

γ : g *or* y

δ : d

ε : e

ζ : z

η : i

θ : th

ι : i

κ : k *or* c

λ : l

μ : m

ν : n

ξ : x *or* ks

o : o

π : p

ρ : r

σ : s

τ : t

υ : y *or* i

φ : f *or* ph

χ : h *or* ch

ψ : ps

ω : o

αι : e

αυ : af *or* av

ει : i

ευ : ef *or* ev

οι : i

ου : ou

γκ : g

μπ : b, mp, *or* mb

ντ : d, nt, *or* nd

τσ : ts

τζ : tz

Resources

While a bibliographic search in most libraries primarily turns up sources about ancient Greek history, philosophy, or art, a number of good books and articles have been written in English about contemporary Greece. There are several sociological studies of rural Greece, and numerous travelers have written about their experiences in rural areas. In addition, there are a few excellent novels set in present-day Greece, and a small number of descriptive books have recently been published. Increasingly, there are translated works of poets such as Cavafy, Seferis, Palamas, and Elytis. Of course, one should also view such classic films as *Never on Sunday*, *Zorba*, and *Z*, as well as more contemporary works by Greek directors.

In Athens several bookstores carry titles in English, but Eleftheroudhakis (on Panepistimiou Street), Kauffmann (on Stadhiou Street), and Pantelides (on Amerikis Street) are the bookstores of choice. In the United States, Greek bookstores can be found in cities such as New York and Chicago, which have large Greek-American populations. The *Athens News* is the primary source of local news for English speakers, and the *Athenian* magazine is Greece's English-language monthly that provides interesting articles on life in Greece. A new bimonthly publication called *Odyssey* is designed for members of the Greek communities living outside the country.

Listed below are sources that I have found most useful in understanding Greek communication and culture.

Modern Greek History

Robert Browning, ed. *The Greek World*. London: Thames and Hudson, 1985.

This book includes essays by an international team of twelve contributors who analyze various facets of Greek life from the classical, Byzantine, and modern periods. It is illustrated with over 300 photographs, drawings, and maps that help the reader understand the deep ties that modern Greeks have with their past.

Richard Clogg. *A Concise History of Greece*. Cambridge: Cambridge University Press, 1992.

Written in a clear, easy-to-follow style and illustrated with numerous photographs and maps, this introduction to the history of modern Greece is essential reading for anyone seeking to gain a background of the historical circumstances influencing Greece today. The book covers the period from the beginnings of the struggle for independence in the late eighteenth century to the present day.

Greece: A Country Study. Washington, DC: American University, 1985.

Part of a series put out by American University for State Department personnel, this extensive description of Greek history, culture, and customs is an invaluable source of information about the country and its people.

David Holden. *Greece without Columns: The Making of the Modern Greeks*. Philadelphia: J. B. Lippincott, 1972.

While tracing the events of Greek history since independence from the Ottomans in the 1820s, the author comments extensively on the Greek character. He provides one of the most lucid descriptions of the Greek way of thinking as he interprets the tumultuous events of Greek politics during a 150-year period. Although the book stops just as democracy is reemerging in Greece following the military coup of 1967, it provides a foundation for understanding the current political situation.

Historical Novels Set in Modern Greece

The Greek word for a novel is *mythistorema*, a word that combines "myth" and "history." The books below represent a few of the many novels based on historical events by modern Greek writers that one can find translated into English. They give the reader a feeling for both the events of the times and the thoughts and emotions of the people during some of the defining moments in recent Greek history.

Dominique Eudes. *The Kapitanios*. Paris: Fayard, 1970.

Providing a rare voice for the Greek Left, the author covers the period dealing with resistance to the Germans during World War II and the civil war that followed. It is written in a lively style and focuses on the problematic and tragic personality of Aris Velouchiotis, a leader in the Greek Left.

Nicholas Gage. *Eleni*. New York: Random House, 1983.

This story, written about the author's own childhood in war-torn Greece during the 1940s, not only provides a heartrending narrative of his mother's life and death, but offers the reader meaningful insight into the inner workings of Greek village society.

Stratis Haviaras. *The Heroic Age*. New York: Simon and Schuster, 1984.

This coming-of-age tale is set in war-torn Greece during the Greek civil war. A group of young, homeless boys travel across a devastated Greek countryside in an attempt to escape the war that is stealing their childhood from them. They find themselves involved in the most brutal fighting of the war as they are caught in the battle for Mt. Grammos.

Stratis Myrivilis. *Life in the Tomb.* Translated by Peter Bien. Hanover, NH: University Press of New England, 1987. Originally written in 1922.

Written by one of Greece's most respected literary figures, the book chronicles a soldier's experiences in trench warfare on the Macedonian front during World War I. The author served as a volunteer in the service of his country from 1912-1922, participating in the Greco-Turkish and Greco-Bulgarian wars and in World War I. By the same author, *The Schoolmistress with the Golden Eyes* and *The Mermaid Madonna.*

Alexandros Papadiamantis. *Tales from a Greek Island.* Translated by Elizabeth Constantinides. Baltimore: Johns Hopkins University Press, 1987.

Twelve short stories set on the author's native island of Skiathos. His writings capture the folkways of Greece with insightful descriptions of traditional island life. Written near the turn of the century, he portrays both the beauty of the land and sea and the extreme hardships of the time, including the ravages of tuberculosis and alcoholism and the plight of women abandoned by their husbands and sons.

Dido Sotiriou. *Farewell Anatolia.* Athens: Kedros Publishers, 1962.

Occurring during Greece's "Asia Minor Catastrophe," this tale is one of paradise lost and shattered innocence. The book tells the story of a poor but resourceful villager born near the ancient ruins of Ephesus who is caught up in the events of late summer in 1922, when two million Greeks were killed or expelled from Turkey by Kemal Atatürk's revolutionary forces.

Personal Accounts by Foreigners Living in Modern Greece

Gillian Bouras. *A Foreign Wife.* Victoria, Australia: Penguin Books, 1986.

An Australian woman marries a Greek man, and after several years of marriage, they take their children and go to live in her husband's small village. She writes of the cultural clash between her own upbringing and the ways of village life. She is regarded fondly by the villagers as something of a curiosity, and they, in turn, become subjects of both her admiration and her perplexity.

Michael Carroll. *Gates of the Wind.* Athens: P. Efstathiadis and Sons, 1983.

An English native looking for the perfect anchorage for his sailing boat decides to build a house on the island of Skopelos in the Aegean. He writes about his friendship with Vangeli, a Greek villager, his involvement in the life of the island, and his gradual integration with the people.

David MacNeil Doren. *Winds of Crete.* Athens: P. Efstathiadis and Sons, 1981.

An American writer provides an account of six years of living on Crete, describing the development of his relationship with the island and its people. He writes candidly yet affectionately about the hospitality and the guile of the people as he endures poverty, illness, and other hardships, emerging from it all with a stronger faith and a sense of optimism.

Peter Levi. *The Hill of Kronos.* New York: E. P. Dutton, 1981.

The author is a scholar who went to Greece in 1963 and over the next fifteen years developed close relationships with numerous Greeks. He writes about the people he meets and the places he visits, providing an interesting perspective on life under the military dictatorship of 1967-74.

Kenneth Matthews. *Memories of a Mountain War.* London: Longman Group, 1972.

Assigned to cover the Greek civil war as correspondent for the BBC, the author provides a brilliant, firsthand account of history as well as his own personal adventures. His descriptions are more often of the experiences of individual men and women than of political and military maneuvers, giving the reader a picture of everyday life during wartime.

Henry Miller. *The Colossus of Maroussi*. New York: Pocket Books, 1975 (originally published by New Editions in 1958).

An account of travels in Greece by a famous author, who traveled extensively throughout Greece during World War II and afterwards. He writes in particular about the light in Greece and the way in which it transforms everything you see.

Dilys Powell. *An Affair of the Heart*. Athens: P. Efstathiadis and Sons, 1983.

The author lived in Greece with her husband, a British classical archeologist, in the 1930s. In this book she chronicles three of her return visits: immediately after the German occupation of World War II, following the Greek civil war, and during a period of reconstruction. She tells the tale of the village of Perachora and its quest for a museum to house the finds of a nearby excavation. In the story she demonstrates her deep knowledge of and indestructible affection for the people of Greece.

Tom Rothfield. *Stranger among Greeks*. Athens: Presfot, 1985.

An English playwright spends the winter on the island of Aegina, which lies close to Athens in the Saronic Gulf. He recounts his own experiences in living as a stranger among the people of this island, and in the process the reader gains a foreigner's perspective on everyday life.

Thurdis Simonsen. *Dancing Girl: Themes and Improvisations in a Greek Village Setting*. Denver: Fundamental Note, 1991.

An American woman's portrayal of her odyssey in a Greek village. The author has spent part of every year since 1981 in Greece, and she recently bought and restored an abandoned peasant house. In the book, she shares what she learned from her experiences and introduces the reader to many interesting personalities.

Sociological and Ethnographic Studies of Modern Greece

Juliet du Boulay. *Portrait of a Greek Mountain Village.* Oxford: Clarendon Press, 1974.

Written by an anthropologist who conducts her fieldwork in a small village on the island of Euboea, this book describes the values that unify the community and traces the related strains that these values impose on village life. This is a valuable study of a community's transition resulting from large-scale migration away from the village.

John Campbell. *Honor, Family and Patronage.* Oxford: Clarendon Press, 1964.

An anthropological study of the Sarakatsani community of shepherds in northern Greece, this book sheds light on many aspects of Greek society at large. The author's discussion of political and social patronage and his analysis of competition and distrust between nonrelated families help explain the tension that exists in Greek society.

Jane Cowan. *Dance and the Body Politic in Northern Greece.* Princeton, NJ: Princeton University Press, 1990.

Greece is a society where most people dance, and in this book the author strips away the fanciful film images of Greek dance associated with *Zorba* and Melina Mercouri to show how dance revolves around expressions of social knowledge and social power.

Jill Dubisch, ed. *Gender and Power in Rural Greece.* Princeton, NJ: Princeton University Press, 1986.

This collection of essays focuses on the position of women in contemporary Greek society and the changes now occurring in both male and female roles in Greece. The authors challenge the conventional view that women in Greece are oppressed and socially inferior, arguing that women exercise power in numerous ways that may not be apparent.

Ernestine Friedl. *Vasilika: A Village in Modern Greece.* New York: Holt, Rinehart and Winston, 1962.

This is a pioneering anthropological study of a small village on the Greek mainland. Chapters cover matters such as the system of dowry and inheritance and the human relations of the family and the village.

Laurie Kain Hart. *Time, Religion, and Social Experience in Rural Greece.* Lanham, MD: Rowman and Littlefield Publishers, 1992.

Based on the observation of daily domestic, ritual, and economic life in rural Greece during the mid-1980s, this book provides an overview of Eastern Orthodox Christianity as it is practiced in a local setting. The author shows clearly the central role of religious practice in contemporary Greek society.

Michael Herzfeld. *The Poetics of Manhood: Contest and Identity in a Cretan Mountain Village.* Princeton, NJ: Princeton University Press, 1985.

The author describes his ethnographic work in a small village in the interior of Crete, the largest of the Greek islands. He writes about how the Cretan shepherds, often caricatured as "goat thieves and knife pullers," define themselves in relation to each other and to the outside world.

Peter Loizos and Evthymios Papataxiarchis, eds. *Contested Identities: Gender and Kinship in Modern Greece.* Princeton, NJ: Princeton University Press, 1991.

This collection of essays by leading anthropologists takes a look at how Greek men and women function within a complex society based on kinship ties. The volume seeks to transcend the traditional portrayals of male and female roles in Greece, looking outside the institution of marriage and family to the other aspects of Greek social life affected by gender expectations.

Irvin T. Sanders. *Rainbow in the Rock: The People of Rural Greece.*
Cambridge: Harvard University Press, 1962.

This book describes the village setting, religion, the role of
women, the village coffeehouse, ceremonies and holy days,
courtship and marriage, and other aspects of Greek rural life
in the early 1950s. During this period of time Greece was
beginning its slow recovery from the devastation of a decade
of war, and Sanders provides insights into the effects of the
German occupation, resistance, and civil war.

Books by Travelers

Kevin Andrews. *The Flight of Ikaros.* London: Penguin Books, 1984.

The author writes of his travels through Greece during the
civil war while studying at the American School of Classical
Studies in Athens from 1947-51. He provides a graphic, frank
account of rural life in Greece during the time. By developing
close relationships with shepherds and farmers, he experiences the passion, warmth, and impatience of the people he
meets in the countryside.

William Davenport. *Athens.* New York: Time-Life Books, 1978.

This book describes the city of Athens by focusing on the
people who live there. With chapter titles such as "A Robust
Appetite for Enjoyment" and "A Passion for Politics," the
author portrays in rich color the Athenians' zest for social
life.

Marc S. Dubin. *Greece on Foot.* Seattle: Mountaineers, 1986.

For those interested in seeing parts of Greece at three
rather than sixty miles per hour, this book provides both the
details of planning your trip and complete directions for fifty
different hikes. Hiking provides an excellent way to meet
people you would never encounter while traveling by car or
bus.

Lawrence Durrell. *The Greek Islands*. London: Penguin Books, 1978.

After living for many years on several of the Greek islands, the author provides a beautifully written description of his favorite places. The book is written as a travel guide, but its tone is personal, and it weaves together history and myth while providing insight into both archeology and geography. His earlier accounts of life in Greece and Cyprus are captured in the famous *Bitter Lemons* and *Prospero's Cell*.

Patrick Leigh Fermor. *Mani: Travels in the Southern Peloponnese*. London: Penguin Books, 1958.

Of English and Irish descent, the author fought during World War II on the Greek mainland and on Crete, where he organized resistance among the Greeks to the German occupation. This travelogue combines scholarship, imagination, and history as the author explores one of the most remote areas of Greece, the Mani, whose people and culture have deep roots in Byzantium. He writes about the feuds, the towers, and the kindness and the hardiness of the people in this beautiful land.

Patrick Leigh Fermor. *Roumeli: Travels in Northern Greece*. London: Penguin Books, 1966.

Here Fermor writes about wedding celebrations among the Sarakatsan shepherds, the monasteries on the high mountainsides, evenings eating around the fire, old men of the villages, and the variety of landscape across northern Greece. Again, he provides the reader with a solid understanding of the history of the region as he describes the people and the landscape.

Nicholas Gage. *Hellas: A Portrait of Greece*. Athens: Efstathiadis Group, 1987.

Written as a travel guide, this book provides far more to the reader than the usual description of sights and sounds of the country. The author's account of the beauty of Greece is complemented by his discussion of the contradictions and tragedies that have characterized Greek history and contemporary society.

Nikos Kazantzakis. *Journey to the Morea*. New York: Simon and Schuster, 1965.

One of the greatest writers of Greece (author of *Zorba* and *The Last Temptation of Christ*) searches for the roots of his own art and being by traveling through the Peloponnese and providing sketches of the places and history he encounters. This book is especially recommended for those who have read some of Kazantzakis's books, as you meet in these pages some of the people who became characters in later writings.

Stuart Rossiter. *Blue Guide to Greece*. Chicago: Rand McNally, first published in 1967 but revised approximately every five years.

Designed for students of archeology, both professional and amateur, this guide is probably the best available one-volume description of the monuments, museums, roads, and facilities of Greece. Since the Greece of today is so closely linked with its classical and Byzantine past, such a guide can greatly facilitate communication with the people you meet on your journeys through the country.

Living in Greece

American Women's Organization of Greece. *Living in Greece*. Athens: American Women's Organization of Greece, 6 Sinopis Street, 1995.

This handbook provides a very useful guide to housing, travel, shopping, dining, customs, and lifestyle in Athens as well as the countryside. Particular attention is given to the concerns of women professionals and women who accompany their spouses to Greece.

Betty Blair. *Sun, Seasons and Souvlaki*. Athens: Chadjinicoli, 1977.

This short book includes seventy-five, single-page descriptions of Greek terms, concepts, and phrases. Ranging from worry beads to kiosks to icons, the author provides an overview of everyday life that is both clever and informative.

Alec Kitroeff. *Greeks That Never Were*. Athens: Hellenic Publications, 1981.

Providing a humorous look at both Greeks and foreigners, this selection of stories appeared in the *Athens Mirror* and the *Athenian* between 1974 and 1989. Kitroeff's stories deal with all aspects of Greek social and political life, from traffic jams to gossip to public works projects. In addition, he makes polite fun of Russian emigrés, German tour leaders, English sportsmen, and American women.

Multi-National Women's Liberation Group. *Foreign Women in Greece*. Athens: Eleftheros Typos, 1984.

This small handbook covers different aspects of living in Greece that are of particular concern to foreign women. It includes chapters on adjustment, citizenship, marriage, health care, education, religious traditions, and cross-cultural children.

William Papas. *Instant Greek*. Athens: American Book and News Agency, 1972.

A best-seller with tourists, this short book offers a tongue-in-cheek description of Greek nonverbal communication that is witty and genuine. The gestures and signs are illustrated, and descriptions are provided in English, French, German, and Greek. While often exaggerated for effect, the overall presentation is amazingly accurate.

Tom Stone. *Greek Handbook*. Athens: Lycabettus Press, 1982.

Written in the form of a dictionary, this is an A-Z phrase guide to "almost everything you want to know about Greece (and are sometimes afraid to ask)." It covers topics from adultery and baptism to women and work. There are often interesting stories that accompany the descriptions of words, and these stories offer the reader a window into life in Greece.

Business Directories

American Hellenic Chamber of Commerce puts out a four-hundred-page directory of U.S. firms established in Greece and others that are represented by branch offices.

Hellenic Industrial Development Bank (ETBA) publishes an investment guide that can be an invaluable source for anyone seeking to do business in Greece.

About the Author

Benjamin J. Broome is a professor of communication at George Mason University in Fairfax, Virginia. He has spent the past fifteen years in a journey among the Greeks, beginning with a teaching job in Athens immediately after graduate school in 1980-81. He has returned to Greece many times to lead intercultural field studies, work with Greek organizations, attend seminars, and travel the mountains and villages of the Greek mainland and islands. In living with Greek families and working with Greek colleagues, he has experienced firsthand the process of building intercultural relationships.

In preparing this book, Professor Broome returned to Greece for eight months, during which he conducted intensive interviews with Greeks, Americans, and Europeans. This book includes a synthesis of his study of Greek culture, his living experience in Greece, his work in the Greek setting, and the interviews he conducted. As it goes to press, he is living and working in Cyprus on a Fulbright grant, carrying out research and conducting problem-solving and conflict-resolution workshops with Greek Cypriots and Turkish Cypriots.

Index

A

B

C